**THE BODY AND THE BOOK**

A KEYSTONE BOOK®

A Keystone Book is so designated to distinguish
it from the typical scholarly monograph that a
university press publishes. It is a book intended
to serve the citizens of Pennsylvania by educating
them and others, in an entertaining way, about
aspects of the history, culture, society, and environment of the state as part of the Middle
Atlantic region.

the body
and the book

Writing from a Mennonite Life: Essays and Poems

Julia Spicher Kasdorf

THE PENNSYLVANIA STATE UNIVERSITY PRESS
UNIVERSITY PARK, PENNSYLVANIA

Library of Congress Cataloging-in-Publication Data
Kasdorf, Julia, 1962–
     The body and the book : writing from a
     Mennonite life : essays and poems / Julia
     Spicher Kasdorf.
          p.   cm.
"Originally published in 2001 by Johns Hopkins University Press."
Includes bibliographical references and index.
Summary: "A collection of essays by poet Julia Spicher
Kasdor focusing on aspects of Mennonite life. Essays
examine issues of gender, cultural, and religious identity
as they relate to the emergence and exercise of literary
authority"–Provided by publisher.
ISBN 978-0-271-03544-4 (pbk. : acid-free paper)
1. Mennonites–Poetry.
2. Poets, American–20th century–Biography.
3. Mennonite women–United States–Biography.
4. Kasdorf, Julia, 1962.
5. Mennonites.
I. Title.

PS3561.A6958B63 2009
811'.54–dc22
2009016613

For Gordon Pradl

Contents

Preface to the 2009 Edition ix

Preface and Acknowledgments xv

I ✍ **A PLACE TO BEGIN**

1 Mountains and Valleys 3

2 Tracking the Mullein, or
Portrait of a Mennonite Muse 9

3 When the Stranger Is an Angel 26

II ✍ **WRITING HOME**

4 Bringing Home the Work 39

5 Preacher's Striptease 48

6 Bodies and Boundaries 75

III ✍ **THE WITNESS A BODY BEARS**

7 Work and Hope 99

8 Marilyn, H. S. Bender, and Me 121

9 The Gothic Tale of Lucy Hochstetler
and the Temptation of Literary Authority 143

IV ✍ **CONCLUSION**

10 Writing Like a Mennonite 167

Afterword 191

Notes 193

Preface to the 2009 Edition

How dreary—to be—Somebody,
How public—like a Frog—
To tell one's name—the livelong June—
To an admiring bog.
                    —Emily Dickinson

"If you want to be a writer," poet Maggie Anderson once told me, "you have to agree to do your growing up in public." She meant the kind of writer who chooses, and is chosen, to publish: "public—like a Frog."

This shot of common sense—and the implied advice to quit fretting and accept the obvious—is especially pertinent as I look at these essays, the oldest published eighteen years ago. On the one hand, I'm grateful that Patrick Alexander and Penn State Press have granted this book a second life in paperback. On the other, I have not entirely overcome the ambivalence about self-disclosure described in the preface of the first edition. I debated whether to follow through with plans to reprint until novelist Rudy Wiebe pointed out another obvious fact: failing to publish an out-of-print university press title will not make the book go away, not with all those copies already shelved in the stacks of college libraries. Reprinting in paperback only makes a book more accessible to a young writer who might be able to use it some day, and so the prospect of being useful to someone trumps shame.

Unlike lyric poems that seem to compose moments outside of time and properly hold them there, personal essays are tentative, contingent, attached to ephemeral objects, everyday anecdotes, and passing thoughts. Only eight years old, this book already feels like the product of another life. Indeed, it is the work of an emerging author under the spell of graduate school, before she moved just thirty miles from the mythic valley described with such longing in these pages, before she became a mother or took up work with graduate students of her own, before 9/11 demonstrated the consequences of one kind of identity politics. I prefer to hold that earnest, young soul at a distance and regard her work with generosity. Her writing is simple yet intense, excessive in imagery, emotion, and imaginative leaps, unaware of many things I could only learn later on about myself and others—poet Di Brandt's exile from her home community, for instance, which I would never now trivialize.

These essays are products of their time, not only in terms of personal life, but perhaps more interestingly with regard to broader conversations about writing and knowledge. During the early 1990s, my friends at NYU were passionately committed to using the first-person singular, which still carried a tantalizing hint of the transgressive. In the Expository Writing program where I worked, Pat Hoy and others had found ways to update expressive pedagogy so that students could make academic arguments with an "I" and employ personal experience as one type of evidence. In those years, an issue of *PMLA* staged a debate about whether dissertations in the humanities should admit the first-person singular, or whether professors should wait to get tenure before publishing personal works. At Duke, Jane Tompkins and Jane Kaplan were already writing scholarly essays and even entire books that began with themselves and yet challenged foundational assumptions in their fields. Our favorite articles often started and ended with the writer located somewhere—sadly, sometimes only at his desk, dutifully mindful of his position with regard to race, class, and gender.

For so long, the experience of women and marginal groups had not contributed to the creation of common knowledge, and we intended to set that to rights. "The personal is political," we intoned. By "political," we meant anything having to do with the workings of power in the world. "Knowledge is power." And knowledge, we knew, is socially constructed and locally situated—that is, personal—and therefore open to critique by those means. As writers, we framed the essential drama—as it also appears in this collection—as a movement from shameful silence into "voice," from the margins into writing for school and writing for ourselves. We cited Adrienne Rich, probably in paraphrase: "You start out writing to save yourself and sometimes you end up saving the whole community."

What grand permission this climate granted to someone from a community that did not value individual authority as much as hard work, humility, and yielding to the good and common cause. I could write my life and help others at the same time. Moreover, the heady confluence of feminism and multiculturalism enabled me to see that a tiny, traditional subculture is not only worthy subject matter for literature, but that I could write from or out of that place, a place that keeps shifting and changing and that may remain static only in my memory. In 1995, when I sent *Mennonite Quarterly Review* a copy of "Work and Hope," an article in this collection that originated in a grad school seminar, the editor reasonably questioned the personal anecdotes at the beginning and end of the piece. I refused to remove them or relegate them to footnotes, insisting that this gesture, which situates my research in the context of individual experience, reveals a *humble* position because it makes no claims to impersonal knowledge. His suggestion may have had nothing to do with pride or epistemology; likely he sought to shape a clean argument uncluttered by the details of my initial visit to the archive or my own struggles as an apprentice digger in the fields of the academy.

Yet I wrote that article, as I wrote the rest of this book, essay by essay, sometimes with great difficulty, not so much to present my findings as to show the ways I found to think and the ways I found to speak. Whether my primary audience was an imagined Mennonite community, members of the Mennonite diaspora, or "the world," I was always my own first reader. I needed this book to exist and it didn't, so I wrote it, supported by the belief that finding voice is always better than silence. (By "voice" I mean articulation—the move to language that transforms experience into verbal forms that can be shared with others.) I love the essays that "show their work," in the words of my eighth-grade algebra teacher, the process more interesting than a flawless scholarly product. Plenty of hard evidence now shows that personal writing benefits the writer; it can help to heal physical and psychic trauma and make individuals more "emotionally literate," that is, better able to recognize and use the forms of knowledge that come by way of feeling.

But then what? Former Goshen College student Clarissa Gaff, in her own essay review of this collection, cited a friend's complaint: "I started out liking the essays, but they always end with her, and they begin to seem so self-centered." At that point, Gaff had had her fill of Kasdorf; she counted three campus visits from this alumnae author during her four years at college, and she'd endured plenty of Kasdorf required reading, too. (How quickly the revolution becomes the counterrevolution.) Still, Gaff has a point. All this personal narrative grounded in the details of gender and sect can become a petite identity politics, where individual claims stem from belonging to and speaking from a group. It gets messy when the aims of one group—feminists, say—conflict with the values of another group, such as the traditional community. The process by which the writer comes to think and speak as she does, constantly disclaiming yet simultaneously claiming her own authority, can seem self-absorbed and even oppressive.

Too often the spectacle of utterance and difference—"To tell one's name—the livelong June"—becomes an end in itself. Because the logic of identity politics generalizes, individual texts get read back onto the group and are valued for their ability to represent the many. Instead, individual texts should invite more personal writing, so that the multitude within the bog becomes fully apparent. To some extent, this has already happened; since the appearance of this collection, the University of Iowa Press published an anthology of Mennonite poetry edited by Ann Hostetler, and Cascadia Press initiated a poetry series by Mennonite writers, edited by Jeff Gundy, also the author of a critical book on the subject. At the same time, I have come to see that public articulation is not *always* better than silence. When it is chosen, silence can be a powerful yet peaceful form of resistance and self-possession.

Once she has learned to pronounce her name and describe her experience, to whom does she listen, in what ways does her mind change again and again, what else can she say? Is "voice," no matter how hard won, ever enough? The hero at the conclusion of this book—figured as a martyr who articulates or bears "good witness" to her experience and then bursts into flame—speaks to realities beyond her own life and place. Her testimony, essential to the formation of a subjective self, also challenges and engages broader conversations.

Personal writing would be "dreary," or merely self-centered, if it did not always emerge from and return to conversation. Personal writing comes from curiosity and uncertainty, attitudes I will always affirm. The dialogue between author and ideas, individuals, traditions, and texts continues to speak beyond the book, beyond the relic or provocation you now hold in your hand.

Do we not turn to memoir and other kinds of personal writing to find language to understand the events of our own lives? Do we not read them with intimate and empathetic desire, always seeking ourselves through the other—no matter what differences we find? I dare to imagine a young writer who might make use of this book some day because I was encouraged and challenged by the personal work of authors as diverse as Virginia Woolf and Madeleine L'Engle. I—we—write and publish these texts not because we want to be "somebody," in Dickinson's terms, but because we seek to create our selves as voices engaged in the conversational stream, and thereby we invite others to come into "voice" by writing, and, yes, by making more books.

Bellefonte, Pennsylvania 2008

Preface and Acknowledgments

Almost a decade ago I drafted "Bringing Home the Work," a short essay that now lies at the center of this collection. It was written in urgency and defensive anticipation of the responses that I imagined Mennonite readers might have to *Sleeping Preacher,* my first book of poems. In those days I was working full-time as a writer of grant proposals at New York University. I knew I was some kind of poet, although at twenty-nine I had little proof of this beyond a handful of magazine publications and a master's degree in creative writing. I knew that I didn't want to sit in front of a computer from nine until five o'clock for the rest of my life, and I knew that I had little interest in only following the theoretical turn that literary studies had taken, so I was enrolled in evening courses in English Education.

In a moment that I cannot forget, I sat nervously on a chair outside the office of Gordon Pradl, the professor of a course in reader response theory that I'd taken. Although I did not know him well, I wanted this teacher's response to the essay on my lap. From the sounds of it, he was on the phone or talking with someone. As my lunch hour slipped away, I remained seated. After about twenty minutes, he finally stuck his head out the door and said, "Oh, I didn't realize you were waiting there. Come in. Why didn't you say something?"

"I didn't want to disturb you," I replied.

And that was true; the injunction to disturb no one—not even oneself—is so deeply ingrained in my Mennonite soul as to be a reflex. Yet I did want to disturb him. I wanted very much to interrupt his day and to let him know that I was there; I wanted to say something to him, anything, many things! In particular, I wanted him to read my essay and to somehow share my anxiety about publishing in the presence of Mennonite readers—family and others who would likely be troubled by what I had written. Of course, I wanted to disturb all of them also, to make them notice what I see and make them understand what I think. I wanted to let them know that I had been there, watching and waiting quietly all of those years—although I could have admitted none of this then. I want to disturb you too, my reader, even as I would like to seduce you sweetly through the pages of this book. Yet I still find myself sitting in that edgy space between not wanting to interrupt and wanting to announce that I am here and that I have many things to tell.

I do not know why Gordon was so attentive to my text and my life that day in his office. Perhaps he was only being the generous teacher he is. Perhaps he was curious about the contradictory student he had known to be capable of thoughtful and effusive writing for assignments but of only faltering talk or stubborn silences in class. In any case, his response was encouraging enough to help me finish the piece, and the conversation begun over that essay continued throughout my doctoral studies and beyond. He has since read drafts or talked with me about the ideas explored in every essay contained in this book.

With the publication of my poetry volume during the early 1990s, I began uneasily to gain a public voice in my home community, and these essays evolved in response to that process. All of my scholarly and creative inquiries into Amish and Mennonite culture and history during the last decade have been part of an attempt to negotiate an authorial identity without either abandoning my home community altogether or becoming silenced by it, a struggle that Gordon Pradl recognized in the earliest essay, "Bringing Home the Work."

When that essay was published in a denominational magazine, an alarmed female reader wrote a letter to the editor stating that she believed I should enjoy the pleasures of being a wife and mother rather than choosing such a dubious vocation. This response showed me that the problem I was trying to solve was not as theoretical as it seemed; it had a sex and a family and a memory. So this book deals with the particular circumstances of one life—its landscape, community, gender, and memory—and also with the ways that growing up Mennonite and female have set what Stanley Fish calls "enabling constraints" on my work as a writer. "The body" in the title thus refers to the religious community—which, following biblical metaphors, figures itself both as "one body" and as the Body of Christ—as well as my own and other bodies in all of their blessed, fallen experience. "The book" refers both to the Bible and to *Martyrs Mirror*—a seventeenth-century compilation of martyr narratives that has been central to Mennonite identity—as well as to the books I might try to write, the books I read, and the massive dictionary, storehouse of words, that appears in the final essay. Throughout this collection I am concerned with the relationships between cultural tradition and innovation, collective history and individual memory, sectarian refusals and cosmopolitan desires; I seek to honor my distinctive Mennonite heritage even as I transgress and transcend its limits.

The first section locates my writing in the old Amish settlement in a valley of Mifflin County, Pennsylvania, my birthplace and the site of childhood memories that stick like glittering splinters in my mind. "Mountains and Valleys" establishes my personal relationship with that landscape and its people and also describes the effect of our family's repeated returns and departures, linking them to my own later visits, which became an important source of vision and imagery in my early work. My parents grew up in Amish and Conservative Mennonite households in that valley, but choices to pursue educational opportunities and professional vocations caused them to migrate from family farms to the western part of the state, where I was raised in an observant Mennonite home yet apart from the rural, religious ethos. The second essay in the first section traces the sources of my work back to that ancestral valley and to a strong-voiced conservative Mennonite woman in that community, but it suggests that writing may be the consequence of wandering as well as devotion to one place and its rich, ancient sources. "When the Stranger Is an Angel" tells the story of an encounter between a roving hobo and my father before the latter had learned to speak English and finds in that tale patterns of engagement with strangers that I would later follow.

The second section takes up some problems that arise when one tries to write out of a traditional ethnic and religious background, particularly as these problems relate to the negotiation of individual and collective identity. Cultural minorities like Mennonites, who carry a memory of persecution and feel their identity to be always endangered, see in the voices of imaginative writers like me the promise of preservation as well as the threat of misrepresentation. "Bringing Home the Work" articulates my fear of the community's reaction to my first poetry collection, outlining some Mennonite resistances to literature as I understood them at the time. "Preacher's Striptease," written eight years after the publication of *Sleeping Preacher,* more fully reflects on my position within a triangle that is formed by the writer, the literary community, and the religious/ethnic community. Anecdotes illustrate my attempts to situate my work in light of the demands and expectations that both communities place on a writer who becomes regarded as an ethnic author. Here I also describe the ways in which writing the essays collected in this book have enabled me to gain some perspective on those expectations and therefore achieve more control over my own representation. A final piece in this section takes up the problem of identity in a Mennonite context, turning to the Russian thinker Mikhail Bakhtin for models of peaceable relationships between group and individual that honor the distinctives of the collective corpus while respecting the boundaries of each of its constituent members.

The essays in the final section use a historical episode as the site to consider voice—spoken and written—and its relationship to both gender and religious tradition, particularly as it concerns the endangered body. "Work and Hope" chronicles the evolution of a seventeenth-century printer's mark. This image and motto are significant because they were absorbed into the canonical text of *Martyrs Mirror*—a compendium that was the first and most important work of Mennonite literature and the largest book of any kind published in the American colonies. The image and motto also reflect an enduring cultural emphasis on labor that continues to haunt me as a writer and thinker. The second essay in this section selects August 1962, and the tragic death of Marilyn Monroe, as vantage points from which to view cultural change in American Mennonite communities. I explore some implications of those shifts for women, particularly in terms of my quest for literary authority. The final essay in this section chronicles a highly publicized incident from the middle of the twentieth century—an Amish bishop who kept his mad daughter chained to her bed—and considers the ways that writers may gain authority by speaking on behalf of silent others.

In the final essay of the collection, I draw together themes that have appeared for some time as explicit and implicit subjects in my writing. Here I describe my childhood relationship with a pedophilic family friend and reflect on the ways that my compliance with and resistance to his attention may have been influenced by my knowledge of the Anabaptist martyr stories. I use these memories to probe the significance of physical violation, memory and forgetting, and individual and collective moves toward gaining a literate voice. Personal narratives in conversation with the community's history help me to understand silence, survival, and the necessity of writing as a means of articulation, integration, and witness for endangered groups.

Editing this collection, I have found that the essays written in Brooklyn while I was still living and working in New York City seem mostly addressed to the Mennonite community, whereas the ones written after I returned to Pennsylvania seem to be about that community—as if written from a vantage point that was slightly removed. Perhaps I had to go back to a familiar landscape and take a job at a college where I would work with Mennonite people to finally clarify and make peace with the tender and intimate distance that will always exist between me and my birthright community. Although some days I still feel Mennonite to the bone, bound to the community by deep ethnic affinities and cultural sensibilities, I have found a spiritual home in the sacramental seasons and worship of the Episcopal Church.

Occasionally, these two worlds meet in brief but illuminating moments. Some time ago, for instance, Canon Peter Greenfield, a retired priest I came to know at St. Stephen's Episcopal Cathedral in Harrisburg, mentioned that for years he had worked in a small parish in Lewistown, Pennsylvania. In fact, he knew folks from the local Mennonite community of Big Valley, including some of my relatives. The difference between Mennonites and Episcopalians, he told me, can be captured in an experience he had at Locust Grove, one of the Mennonite meetinghouses in that valley. One day as he and several of his parishioners were attending a meeting there, an Episcopalian noticed that in the large sanctuary devoid of nearly all decoration, a large circle hung on the wall above the pulpit. "What do you suppose that means?" the man asked his priest. Peter replied that the significance of a circle must be similar for all Christians—suggestive of God's eternal presence, Alpha and Omega, divine mystery without beginning or end—but he did ask the Mennonite pastor when he had a chance.

"Oh that," the pastor replied. "The builders put it there to hide a ventilation duct."

I love this story because I admire the Episcopalian sense of the symbolic and ornamental as much as the Mennonite instinct for the useful and bluntly true. Moreover, I know that Peter and his parishioners were in a Mennonite meetinghouse that day because they had volunteered to help their Mennonite and Amish neighbors operate the Mennonite Central Committee's meat canner. Created in the middle of the twentieth century to assist World War II refugees, this contraption on a flat-bed truck traveled to thirty-three communities in twelve states and in Ontario, Canada, to process more than 220 tons of meat during its 1999–2000 season. Each year, at each location, butchers and farmers from Anabaptist-related groups donate beef cattle, turkeys, and pigs, and volunteers supply labor. And the marvel of the canner, Peter told me, is that nothing is wasted. In fact, my own great-aunt Twila—whom he met working with the project—would not allow him to discard anything, not bones that could be boiled for broth, not fat that could be made into soap or fed to the birds. Perhaps the canner does not comply with the most sophisticated or efficient plans for combating world hunger, but it satisfies a basic human need to do something concrete in the face of cruel and confusing times; it enables an Iowa hog farmer to offer some of his pork to families in Sudan, Bosnia, Serbia, Haiti, North Korea, Russia, Iraq, and Kosovo. In Mennonite farm communities, people say that they are slaughtering their animals or offering their labor "for relief," meaning that they believe that they are helping to relieve the suffering of others. But I am sure that they also gain some relief themselves from the shared work and sense of satisfaction that comes when the canner truck rolls out of town.

So in the spirit of the meat canner, I offer these essays. They are composed for relief from whatever was at hand in my life: memory, stories, treasures, trauma, and the need to make meaning out of loss and change. I send them, bound in a book, to strangers. Nor have I written them alone. I am especially thankful for conversations with the many Anabaptist and Mennonite people and institutions that have helped me. I think of Laura Weaver, who first asked if I would ever publish "Bringing Home the Work" in a more permanent form, and of Lois Frey and Julie Musselman, who have been valuable discussion partners through the years. John Ruth, author, filmmaker, and preacher, deserves special thanks because he appears to be such a troublesome figure in this book; without his provocations and memory, I would have a weaker voice. Rudy Wiebe, another Mennonite literary precursor, has been enormously generous and supportive. Scholars Hildi Froese Tiessen and Ervin Beck nurture Mennonite literature on both sides of the U.S.-Canadian border with their writing and conference planning, and Ervin applied his critical wits to a large portion of this manuscript. Joe Springer, curator of the Mennonite Historical Library in Goshen, Indiana, has rescued me more than once from my bungling. Poet Jeff Gundy and preachers John D. Rempel and Scott Holland remain dear friends and trusted readers.

I could not have finished this book without the support of Messiah College, including release time from my teaching duties, financial support, technical assistance from David Owen, Dennis Hose, and the superb editing skills of Cherie Fieser. Messiah students Joy Yu-Ho Wang and Carmen McCain read the entire manuscript and provided comments that were useful in revision, as did my colleague Helen Walker; Sarah Todd helped to research and secure copyright permissions. George F. Thompson and Randall Jones at the Center for American Places, copyeditor Elizabeth Yoder, and Juliana McCarthy at the Johns Hopkins University Press were very helpful during the revision and production process. Fellow New York University graduate students Marylou Gramm and Jennifer McCormick offered useful responses to some of these essays, and writers Nicole Cooley and Donald Antrim gave me advice and encouragement in moments when I faltered. Peter Powers was a thoughtful reader and car pool partner during the years when I was working on this collection. As always, I owe an immeasurable debt to David Kasdorf, whose enduring belief in my work and in my life helps to sustain them both.

I am thankful to the magazines and journals in which some of these essays were previously published, often in slightly different forms. Chapter 1 appeared as "Mountains, Valleys, and a Place to Begin," *Central PA* (Oct. 1999): 23–24, and was reprinted in *Now and Then: The Appalachian Magazine* 14.3 (1998). Chapter 3 was published in the *Conrad Grebel Review* 12.2 (1994): 197–201. Chapter 4 appeared as "Bringing Home the Work: Thoughts on Publishing a First Book," in *Festival Quarterly* 19.1 (1992): 7–10. Chapter 6 was published as "Bakhtin, Bodies, and Boundaries" in the *Mennonite Quarterly Review* 71.2 (1997): 169–88, and Chapter 7 as "Work and Hope: Tradition and Translation of an Anabaptist Adam," in the *Mennonite Quarterly Review* 69.2 (1995): 178–202.

The following institutions and individuals provided contexts and conversations that were essential to the creation and revision of several essays, and I am indebted to those who planned and organized them: Ervin Beck and the 1997 "Mennonite/s Writing in the U.S." conference at Goshen College; Susan L. Biesecker-Mast and Gerald Biesecker-Mast and the 1998 "Anabaptists and Postmodernity" conference at Bluffton College; Nicole Cooley and the "Writing Across

Communities: Genre, Audience, and Identity" panel at the 1998 Associated Writing Programs conference in Albany, New York; Scott Holland and the 1993 Laurelville Mennonite Church Center conference on Narrative and Theology; and the Bluffton College Forum Lectures.

I

A PLACE TO BEGIN

Mountains and Valleys

1 Scientists believe that human beings first stood up and began walking on the Serengeti Plain, but I cannot shake my sense that life began in a valley. In my imagination, the Garden of Eden is bounded by mountains that are as green and worn as those of the Appalachian Ridge in Central Pennsylvania, where a gradual, prehistoric collision of two continents created peaks that were once as high as the Himalayas. Now they form gentle shapes with names like "Jack's" or "Standing Stone," which are known simply as "Front Mountain" and "Back Mountain" by those who live between them in the Kishacoquillas Valley, south of State College and north of Lewistown.

The inhabitants of that fertile valley—about thirty miles long and no more than five miles wide at its lower end and two miles wide at the upper end—call it "Big Valley" or simply "the Valley." They draw their bearings from ridges: Back Mountain is not quite north, and Front Mountain is nearly south. Actually, the Valley does not run true to the compass at all, so the sun always rises and sets slightly askew. When they leave, former residents struggle with a shaky sense of direction for the rest of their lives. They always consider themselves to be from the Valley, no matter how long they've lived elsewhere or how far from tradition and family they've traveled.

I do not know when I first came to love the Valley. Perhaps its dairy farms and forested ridges inscribed themselves on my consciousness as soon as my eyes grew strong enough to see beyond the arms of my mother. As a gosling will claim for a parent whatever barn cat wanders into view, I fixed my gaze on the land that had fed, sheltered, worried, and buried the bodies of my ancestors for generations. According to legend, Amish settlers sailing up the Susquehanna and Juniata rivers in the 1790s could tell by the taste of spring water when they had found limestone soil. They were immigrants and the children of immigrants who had made the Atlantic crossing prior to the American Revolution, fleeing European laws that forbade them freedom to worship or baptize according to their beliefs, to abstain from war, to own land, or to bury their dead in church cemeteries.

My parents were the first in each of their families to leave farms in Big Valley, although there are stories from every generation about ones who "went West." At an outdoor reception after a cousin's wedding, I complained to one of my plain-dressed great-aunts about the clear-cut lumbering that has left hideous scars on mountainsides that we could see that day from the lawn. "You like these mountains?" she eyed me doubtfully through rimless glasses. "You know, *Daadi* didn't love the mountains like we do. That's because he grew up in Nebraska." Great-grandfather Yoder was born in an Amish community that had migrated from Juniata County and eventually failed in a prairie drought. An adventurer, he'd stopped at the 1893 Chicago World's Fair on his way back to a Pennsylvania landscape he could not have fathomed, growing up on the flat lands. He died an old man in Big Valley—where he is still remembered as remarkably thoughtful and cosmopolitan for a man who plowed with mules—perhaps still chafing at the confines of landscape.

Although my parents moved away from the Valley before my first birthday, I always regarded it as our real home, more home than the scrappy hills of western Pennsylvania where I was growing up among grandchildren of mill workers and miners. Our theology implies that Mennonites are strangers and pilgrims, but I knew that there was one place on this earth where we would always belong. We returned often to observe those occasions that bind individuals to history and kin—weddings, funerals, family reunions—and always the mountains received us in an ambiguous embrace. Driving through what people call "the tight end," barely wide enough for narrow Route 655, my father would moan, "Oh, the mountains." Or, "It's like returning to the womb." And my mother would gently retort, "John, it's stifling."

Savoring this ritual from the back seat, slightly carsick, I learned to associate mountains with meanings that reach beyond timber and rock to the boundaries of human community. I learned to connect a certain queasiness with limits, and to love and resist them as my parents did. Out of respect for traditional relatives, I always wore dresses with sleeves on those visits, having learned early to accommodate a conservative code of dress and behavior. I regarded that world with a nostalgia unusual in children who are too young to have lost very much. At ten or twelve, I sat alone on a bus headed west on Route 22, clutching a gallon milk jar that I'd planted with tea berries, mosses, and a small hemlock, during a visit to the Valley. Every so often, I lifted the lid of what my great-aunts called "the winter garden" and took a long breath of the mountains, letting the moist scent of melancholy flood my lungs. Already, a mystical valley had been carved within me, forged by a stream of desire—my own and the longings of Amish and Mennonite kin who wanted me always to belong there, to belong among them, although I was clearly growing up outside.

Once when I was playing in the creek that runs past my grandparents' place in the Valley, a milk truck stopped on the bridge. The driver called to me, guessing that I must be a "Fresh Air." I knew what he was talking about—every African-American or glamorous worldly child in my grandparents' snapshot album had been transported from New York City by the Fresh Air Fund. These outsiders feared cows and country darkness; they grew inexplicably homesick for crowded apartments and sweltering streets, though some of them came to love the Valley. A pair of girls from the South Bronx returned to my grandfather's place every summer for six or seven years during the 1950s. When I moved to New York City myself in the 1980s, Bertha, my great-aunt and step-grandmother, urged me to get in touch with those twins, grown up now and living in New Jersey, but I never did.

"No!" I shouted indignantly to the man in the milk truck, incensed that he'd guessed I did not belong to that valley. "I'm not a Fresh Air! I'm John and Virginia's daughter!" At some point, I'd already learned that being related to people can make you belong to a place. Land, when it has sustained families for generations, does not easily let go of a body.

I realized this again several years ago, climbing out of a car at the MacDowell artists colony in New Hampshire, states away from where I was born, as the scent of hemlock woods and newly mown hay rushed into my lungs and struck something behind my sternum: the valley within me, my inspiration. That summer I finished *Sleeping Preacher* in a landscape that kept Big Valley and its people at the center of my imagination, even though I was living far away, laboring among practicing artists, not farmers. I wrote poems to remember those mountains but also to cross them so that they would not always be barriers dividing my life between the place where I was born and the world where I had chosen to roam. I sought words to name a place where eloquent language is suspect because the deepest meanings are conveyed in silence among kin—a sack of potatoes left on the doorstep by a neighbor, a hand pressed in sympathy after a death. I wrote for myself and for those who are made uneasy by mountains, who love them because they give gorgeous form to the land and who hate them because they get in the way. Mountains set limits, mark endings and beginnings, and remind us that only when one crosses them can one look back and begin to see the place she has come from.

Now I live less than a two-hour drive from the Valley, and my great-aunts complain that they saw more of me when I lived in New York City than they do now that I've moved back to Pennsylvania. It's true.

THAT STORY

In this story, the Garden of Eden is the Valley;
Adam and Eve are the parents who left
all those fine Holsteins and the swallows
darting under the barn beams at dusk.
Once out of the Garden, they had to find jobs,
so Eve became a nurse, silent witness to the world's ills,
and Adam was doomed to office work. In the evenings
he pushed a plow in his garden's poor soil,
while his children stooped over the furrows
behind him, trailing pebbles of fertilizer
from their fists, dropping seeds
painted pesticide pink.

In this story, Cain is a woman
who slays with words. She moves to the city
where she fusses over a Christmas cactus and
African violets in pots. Her garden is only as wide
as a sidewalk; stray cats pee on her ragged
tomato stalks. Sometimes she thinks back to the nights
she and her father, tired together, sat
on the edge of their patch. Now she knows
his silent longing for that Garden.
It is easy to believe that story
and to grow as weary
as Israel's children
by the waters of Babylon.

When I lived in New York, I relished long train trips from the city on the old Pennsylvania line that traced my ancestors' migration up the Susquehanna from Harrisburg to the Juniata River, then into the mountains and valleys, where someone would always meet me at the small train station in Lewistown, place of my birth. Or on the return trip, I loved the last moments as the locomotive broke from the New Jersey tunnel and emerged into light and Manhattan's sheer, womb-like walls of cement and glass, just before it entered Penn Station to release passengers into the swarming tunnels at 34th Street. Once during those years, as they were waiting for a train to pass in front of their automobile, my young nephew Jason asked his mother, "Is this Julia's house?" He had seen me step from a train onto the platform at the Lancaster station so many times that he was certain I lived in an Amtrak passenger car.

Now I wonder whether what invigorated me most during the trips between the city and central Pennsylvania was not an arrival at either end but the suspension of the demands that either destination placed on me. I liked being able to think in the free space between places, and the ways that my own travel could make a connection between them. Aristotle believed that the true sign of a philosopher's intuition is his ability to find similarities in things that are different, the making of metaphors. As poetry's power often comes from linking two unlike things to release new insight, so my life has been charged by the experience of embodying a connection between disparate locations. From childhood, I learned to love the anticipation of arrival and also to follow a road between the traditional community and the non-Mennonite world. Now that distance is not as great as it once seemed. Yet in writing and in life, I continue to both seek and flee the complicated embrace of landscape, community memory, and family, singing the drama of loss and desire as I go.

CAMP HILL, 2000

Tracking the Mullein, or
Portrait of a Mennonite Muse

2

Although he now claims that he cannot recall it, Mennonite author and preacher John Ruth once told me that he thinks I am like the mullein, which will spread its woolly leaves and send up a giant stalk of banana-colored flowers any place, even in the mortar of a log house, and no one can tell where it came from. I believe he intended the remark as a compliment, but I could not avoid hearing in it shades of a familiar, skeptical query: Where does her voice really come from? How did a flashy yellow flower get to that dry spot on the roadside—by underground root? on the wind? inside the body of a bird or bat?

Increasingly, it has felt necessary to explain my position in relation to the conservative Mennonite and Amish people from central Pennsylvania portrayed in my first book. Some who belong to that community and who recognize themselves or their stories in my poems may accuse me of dishonesty and arrogance, of shamelessly dragging out dark tales and half-truths that should have been left to rest. Those who know more about poetry than about Mennonite life regard the book mostly in terms of its ability to represent an American subculture. A few Mennonite intellectuals who move somewhere between the traditional community and the wider world—those closest to my own position—enjoy clarifying my visitor status on the family farm. They wonder if I am entitled to tell the stories I have told and suspect that I have simply crafted a marketable fiction of identity for myself.

I would rather not respond to these irksome charges that usually come to me secondhand. I know that it is impossible and perhaps even unwise for a writer to try to track the sources of her work, because they are so deeply embedded in the journey a life takes, springing from all of its conversations and experiences. For the sake of this essay, though, I will spin a myth of origins, while hastily admitting that such singular claims of authenticity must always be false. Perhaps it will be a satisfying story, nevertheless, bypassing the complicated travels of real life and simply beginning at a place that, in my imagination, is inextricably bound to one person, my Mennonite muse.

I start with the Ridge and Valley region of central Pennsylvania, where about two hundred years ago my ancestors established farm settlements in Juniata and Mifflin counties. Of course, the most beautiful and fertile valley in that region is my ancestral home, Big Valley, defined by Front Mountain and Back Mountain, which pinch together to create a slightly curved earthen pod between Tight End and The Narrows. (Although everyone knows these names for the landscape, you will not find them on maps.)

Forsaking the land for educational and vocational opportunities of mid-twentieth-century America, my parents chose to trade farm labor—known to be honorable and supportive of family and community relationships—in exchange for lives they would invent near Irwin, about three hours west of the Valley. They chose this spot because a few Mennonite families already lived in the area and because it was set midway between my father's job in the research laboratories of Westinghouse and the established Mennonite community at Scottdale. I now believe that my father deliberately chose to locate our family on the edge of a small town—not in a suburban-style housing plan—because he wanted land enough for large vegetable gardens, following rural instincts for thrift and the necessity of keeping young hands occupied with useful work during the summer. When I was young, I also spent summer weeks in the Valley with grandparents, cousins, great-aunts, and great-uncles. That was my only claim on that place as I grew up as part of the larger American improvisation, enrolled in public schools among children of factory and office workers, mostly Catholics of Italian and Eastern European descent. Having shed the distinctive clothing and language of their past, my parents instilled in my brothers and me an ideology of cultural and religious difference that was invisible but keen.

Consequently, as far back as I can recall, I belonged to several places, but I always felt slightly different, not quite a part of wherever I was. This may be one reason I began compulsively to narrate my life in school tablets, the way the nineteenth-century lives of Laura and Mary Ingalls were recorded in the books my mother faithfully read to us during the long afternoons at home before I was old enough to go to school. Even before I could write, I described my activities aloud, embellished with details borrowed from Laura's frontier, until my cousins once caught me talking to myself and teased me without mercy. From fifth grade on, every night, even at slumber parties or on the bathroom floor of a motel room I shared with the rest of my family, I shaped whatever had happened that day into words. In order to

Bertha Peachey Spicher Sharp, studio portrait for the congregational directory of Locust Grove Mennonite Church, taken in the mid-1980s.

have something to write each evening, I developed the habits of watching and of converting experience into language. Travels between the Valley and western Pennsylvania helped me to do this: the Valley made my Catholic playmates in western Pennsylvania, with their fancy sweater sets, seem strange and worthy of note, even as those girls with elaborate last names made my plain relatives seem strange. I was always writing to fill in the space between difference.

Most memorable to me among the plain relatives was Bertha, a Conservative Conference Mennonite spinster who had married my Amish grandfather. In addition to becoming my father's step-mother, Bertha was my mother's aunt, and as a young woman she had worked on my grandparents' farm when my mother was born. Bound to me by marriage, memory, blood, and sex, Bertha gave me a training in the ways of the Valley that was more deliberate than anything she offered to my farm cousins who actually lived there and participated in its culture. Now I see that her attention to me may have been unfair to my farm cousins and likely was motivated by a fear that I might forget where I'd come from or fail to learn who we are. Sufficiently infrequent to attract the attention due an exile, my summer visits with Bertha and others in the Valley lasted long enough for me to attend Bible school at more than one Mennonite church, and Bertha made sure that I did. Those summers, I also learned the stories and lessons stored in her catch-all memory, which reached to the nineteenth century. She taught me how to hang wash on a line so that underwear can't be seen from the road; how to make soap out of lard, lye, and ash; and how to put what she called "the bite" into homemade root beer, using only yeast, sugar, and sunshine.

Listening to Bertha speak Pennsylvania German on the phone or at market, I understood enough to know that she always referred to me as John and Virginia's daughter. She was known by the names of the men with whom she belonged: Jonas's Bertha and also Tom Peachey's Bertha. My great-grandfather, Tom Peachey, her father, who had died felling a tree on Front Mountain, was an auctioneer and loud like the Peacheys. Bertha had a loud voice too, especially noticeable when she

Bertha, with her siblings at the Mifflin County farm near Back Mountain where she grew up and later farmed with my paternal grandfather, Jonas Spicher. From left to right: Joseph, Bertha, Elsie, and Thomas Peachey, my maternal grandfather, in 1918.

sang off-key in church. Years later, her few extravagant phone calls delivered to my ear a voice so shrill that it seemed she believed she had to shout over the mountains all the way from Pennsylvania to my apartment in Brooklyn.

Bertha's voice was so loud because she had lost hearing in one ear when she fell off a silo. As a girl, she'd climbed up there with her older brother Joe, both of them curious to see what the barnyard looked like from above, but she slipped on a ladder rung. When she pulled off her bonnet, it was soaked with blood. I never asked if she went to a doctor or what her mother said; I only imagined a little girl who must have been something like me, determined to see from afar the farmyard and fields that lay every day at her feet. She told me this story often to ensure that I would remember it as I have.

She also told me many times about a little gold dish that she used to serve jelly, although mostly it stayed in its spot in the china closet. She'd sometimes point to that place and say, "You know about that little gold dish?" Then she would tell how she once decided to run

Bertha, second from right, with teachers from the summer Bible school at Flint,
Michigan, in 1938. The dark cape dresses and head coverings indicate that all of
the female teachers belong to the Mennonite Church. Although she rarely wore a
cape in her later years, in 1990 Bertha was buried in a navy dress similar to these,
at her request.

away from home. She'd walked across the fields as far as the Swarey
farm and there found the people cleaning out the attic, so she stopped
to help. For that, the Swarey mother gave Bertha a square dish pressed
from golden-brown glass. When she finally returned home, the dish
was evidence that she had run off, and her own mother punished her.
Eventually, Bertha gave me the little gold dish.

Also in her china closet was a beaded velvet pincushion that pro-
claimed itself to be a souvenir of the Ozarks. Before she married, Bertha
had kept house for a pastor's family at a mission outpost in Arkansas
and taught Bible school in Flint, Michigan: two acceptable but significant adventures for a single woman of her time and faith. Not long
ago, after a poetry reading at Goshen College in Indiana, a middle-
aged woman clasped my hand and said, "You know, I loved Bertha
too." The daughter of that Arkansas pastor then told me part of the
story that Bertha had never revealed: how she had gone South to cook
for a construction team and toward the end of their short stay had

boldly offered to remain behind. Bertha told the pastor's wife that she wouldn't pray in public or teach Sunday school but that she knew how to keep house and care for children. In exchange for room and board, Bertha would do those things so the pastor's wife would be free to do the work of the church. I love to think of the complexity of this plain, young woman cleverly or desperately transforming a brief visit into an extended stay away from home, her refusal to use her own loud voice publicly—in keeping with her religious tradition—and her sense that her labor could free another woman from domestic duty.

Before she married my buggy-driving grandfather, Bertha taught him how to maneuver the shiny, black mound of her 1950s sedan. Thereafter, she rode on the passenger side. Such were the pragmatic and contradictory negotiations that she made all her life. Some other meaning always danced beneath the smooth surface of public appearances, and I never considered her to be especially subjugated because of her gender or religious commitments. So when I requested the believer's baptism to formally join the Mennonite Church in 1976, I decided also to join the diminishing number of women in our congregation who still wore head coverings for worship. My mother took me to Big Valley, where a pastor's wife sold coverings from an extra room built onto the house. I recall walls from floor to ceiling lined with shelves holding orderly stacks of countless sizes and shapes of the tulle caps, some with strings and some without strings, some as big and deep as football helmets, some as flat as clam shells. After much deliberation, I chose a small one edged with lace to wear at my baptism and for worship thereafter.

Some Mennonites found it incongruous to pin a prayer covering onto short hair, and mine had been cut since kindergarten, when my mother had grown weary of my shrieking each time she tried to pull a brush through my curls. Nevertheless, I chose to wear a head covering to gain the approval of my plain relatives and also as a sign of identification with them. Knowing Bertha as I did, the little cap didn't suggest subordination to me, and I assumed I could simply ignore the doctrine of male headship and female submission that it officially signified. Especially did I dismiss editor-clergyman Paul Erb's statement in the official doctrine book that I studied for church membership: "A covering on the head of a bold, boisterous, bossy woman, because it would be inconsistent, would mean nothing."[1] Bertha wore a covering every day, and she was as bold and boisterous as any half-deaf auctioneer's daughter could be, and bossy too. Even from beyond the grave, she bossed us with little handwritten notes taped to the back of her china closet and dresser, directing the destiny of heirlooms.

In August 1990 my father phoned one sunny afternoon to tell me that Bertha had died of a heart attack after being rushed to the hospital in Lewistown, where I'd been born twenty-seven years earlier. I wanted to take the next train to Pennsylvania, but he told me to wait until morning, so I hung up the phone and cleaned our Brooklyn apartment, crying. I cleaned because I know you should never leave a dirty house when you go out of town, and because scrubbing grease from the stove top was all I could think to do.

Later, I realized that I was not suffering the loss of the only old woman I'd ever loved with my whole heart, a fierce woman who could judge and demand, who had a bossy streak as wide as the valley she came from but who could also love you wordlessly through the baking of wild hickory nut cake. I was not grieving the loss of her sun-speckled arms and her black hair barely streaked at eighty, pinned back in a bun under a prayer covering. Not the loss of her fine print dresses, all cut over the same plain pattern, cover-up aprons of another floral print. Not the chunky black oxford shoes and pocketbook, woolen head scarves, rubber galoshes, or steel-rimmed glasses like Malcolm X used to wear. Not the way she held on to me when we embraced, tightly and awkwardly, or her letters of loopy handwriting that always began like an epistle of Saint Paul, "Greetings in Jesus' name," and continued with menus of meals she'd cooked for company, work she'd done in the garden, and the names of those in the Valley who had died the previous week. I now see that her letters were often little more than lists of things, like the details that rush in and threaten to overwhelm whatever I try to write about her: language that is as simple and unequivocal and serviceable as most of her gestures.

I feared that, with Bertha's death, I had lost what she always had been—my link to the Valley, keeper of its stories, guide and teacher of its ways, cook of its foods—my Mennonite muse. Through her I'd learned to love the land that had sustained my ancestors for so long it now feels like part of my own flesh. She had bound me to that place by teaching me how to understand its knowledge through the stories of our predecessors. When I grieved her death, cramming African violets onto my window sills as she would have, I grieved the loss of that valley and its people as they were mediated to me through her memory. But just as Bertha knew how to take fat, ash, and lye and make it into something as useful as soap, I learned that no matter how deep and silencing a grief may seem, writing can transform loss into abundance. I think of the Israeli poet Yehuda Amichai, once so exasperated with the efforts of our graduate poetry workshop that he shouted, "You do not write the poem of love in the night of love! That is the night of love, so you love! You write the poem of love afterward, when love is gone and all you have left is your poetry." Or I think of Hêlêne Cixous, who has observed that some writers need a death close at hand in order to appreciate life and to finally flourish as authors. The guilt a successful writer sometimes feels may come from a sense that the loss of a life or of an entire people has also been her gain.[2]

With Bertha gone, I wrote in a more concentrated and conscious way about the Valley, telling the stories I knew and exploring a range of ambivalent feelings within them. Sometimes I wrote with nostalgia, longing for some glorious thing that never existed, sometimes in shame, sometimes in anger blunted with pain. The poems were full of fragments and odd details—several of them inaccurate, I would later learn. But like Salman Rushdie, the Indian-born author writing in Britain, I realized that the mind sorts and makes its own selections and that the incomplete nature of memory makes whatever we recall all the more meaningful. For him, "the shards of memory acquired

WHERE WE ARE

Bertha let me run barefoot those weeks
at her house. I learned Bible verses
and picked red-stem peppermint from cow creeks
for the tea she steeped in milk jugs.
Thor stem we hung to dry in the attic
for Grandpa's stomach. She called flies
the Mister and Misses we mustn't let in
through the breeze way where *Fleissig Lizzies*
bloomed in the windows. In the cellar
she peeled peaches while steam clattered the lid
of a speckled canner, and I scampered
behind her, "Three guesses, where am I?"
And she'd guess, "Under the steps? Behind
the jam closet? Back of the box of cans
Daddy should dump off the mountainside soon?"
But I'd be in the dark root cellar, crouched
with sprouting potatoes under shelves of jars
that reached to the ceiling: three kinds of pickles,
green and wax beans, red, white, and sour cherries,

greater status, greater resonance, because they were *remains;* fragmentation made trivial things seem like symbols, and the mundane acquired numinous qualities."[3] I dedicated *Sleeping Preacher* to Bertha, who appears as a central figure in many of the poems. Yet I know that I could not have done this if she had not died.

John Ruth once told me that my poems do the work of mourning, providing language for Mennonite people caught in the process of cultural assimilation who don't know how to mourn in an articulate way or who even may not recognize exactly what they have lost. At first I was flattered by this grand statement of purpose and usefulness, and then I felt vexed—as is often the case with things this man tells me. Do I want to spend my one and only life grieving the demise of a

and the horrible beef canned in its tallow.
Three guesses, where am I? Her letters still find me
on paper printed with birds and Bible verses
she writes, "Greetings in Jesus' name.
Come for a weekend, a week. And we must thank God
you will not stay in that city forever."
Instead, I thank God I can still find her
poking her pots of African violets or bent
over the counter, crimping the crust on a pie.
She's still there in that silence, bowing her head
before meals, breathing desirous prayers
or remembering how she flew home to us,
Grandpa's corpse hidden deep in the plane,
how from takeoff to landing she stitched
garlands of daisies on quilt blocks,
her needle tacking black knots on the blooms,
so wherever I use this quilt,
I'll see those seeds and think of Grandpa.
Yet it's her I see, hunched in the soft spot
of airplane light, embroidering above him, alive.

traditional, patriarchal, insular subculture? Why must even my writing, that most excessive and self-indulgent enterprise, be converted into an instrument for community service? Besides, the best grief does not cling to things the way I gathered African violets after Bertha's death or the way some contemporary Mennonites hang old quilts on walls like widows refusing to disburse their dead husbands' clothing and tools. Mourning means burying the dead so that one can move on, enriched with memory yet unencumbered as the mullein shouting up its plentitude of yellow bloom. "Loss is your muse," John Ruth's neighbor, Julie Musselman, told me, and perhaps she was closer to the truth.

If Bertha were still alive, I could never have published that book, and especially not have dedicated it to her, without incurring her disapproval and wrath. I would never have presumed to define the complexities of her affections or to project my own meanings onto her life. If she were able to boss in her own voice—and not just the voice of my conscience or community's memory—I know she would tell me that a weed is not something to celebrate. It is something to yank out of your garden and throw onto the mulch pile to wither. She would say that the little gold dish means nothing about gaining your treasure— as well as punishment—by running away, nothing about returning with a story to tell and thereby redeeming your transgression by some miracle of grace. No, the little gold dish was never intended to grant me permission to move to New York City, the place she refused to visit, insisting instead that one day I would return and settle in one of two counties in central Pennsylvania: Snyder or Union.

Now living down river from those counties, having returned to the landscape of my longing, I find little comfort in the folds of these beautiful old mountains. If anything, I am more determined than ever to keep moving—as Bertha traveled in her childhood and youth, and as the mullein mysteriously travels these roadsides.

When I sent John Ruth an earlier draft of this essay, he insisted that the mullein is not a weed as I'd assumed: "It's a plant—which the people around here respected and gathered for such a spectrum of herbal benefit that its local name was *Woolgraut* (Pennsylvania Dutch for the German *Wohlkraut* [well plant]), a kind of all-round herb which enhances well-being. Old Willy Freed of Vernfield, in his last years, asked me to find some to soak his feet in."[4] I like to think of John collecting mullein leaves and of that old Mennonite fellow, his life's journey nearly complete, soaking his weary feet in that tea.

Another mullein cure is inscribed in the back of the 1948 diary that was kept by my Amish grandmother, Rachel Yoder Spicher. A thirty-eight-year-old farm wife and mother of five, she had time to keep a diary that year because she was bedfast with tuberculosis. Although she

Great Mullein, *Verbascum thapsus.*

spoke only Pennsylvania German at home, each day she made brief, several-lined entries in her written language, English. They record the weather and the almost-daily visits from relatives and friends, and they trace the seasons by following changes in labor around the farm. Occasional sparks of observation glow amidst the meager details of domestic and agricultural life, such as the entry for March 21: "Unusually warm for this time of year. Bees were out today and yesterday." The back pages include lists of the titles of novels and religious and devotional books that Rachel read during her illness and also this recipe for her cure:

> Remedy for Tuberculosis:
> Take 1 handful mullein leaves,
> put in gallon crock and fill half full of alfalfa.
> Pour full of boiling water.
> Drink hot or cold with meals from 3 to 6 months according to
>   your condition.
> Gather the tea before July 1st if possible.[5]

Perhaps the mullein remedy worked. By mid-summer, Rachel was out of bed; consequently, the diary entries thinned, then disappeared altogether. In August 1948, she was killed by injuries sustained in a roadside horse and buggy accident. A few years after her death, my grieving grandfather married Bertha to care for his young children.

Before the European settlers brewed mullein leaves for a cure, American Indians in these parts lined their moccasins with mullein leaves to keep out the cold; and colonists, following their example, slipped the woolly leaves into their stockings.[6] So the leaves of the mullein continued to travel with human feet even after the plant had rooted. Moreover, the mullein has the ability to sprout from almost any part of its organism, and, like the chrysanthemum, it is a genus that freely and endlessly develops new species.[7]

I love the paradox of this flower, both steadfast and capable of movement and change, fastened and free. Because it is rooted, its travel seems all the more strange and meaningful, the way that Bertha's view of her farmstead from the top of the silo was strange, and the ways that her running to the next farm or to the Ozarks now seem significant to me. Yet the mullein can be capable of enormous allegiance to one spot, as John Ruth tells elsewhere in his letter to me, relating a story of root and wing so profound and so nearly devoid of interpretation that it could be a dream:

> Speaking of mulleins, as a boy I had an experience with one that grew up near the road going past our house. For some reason I had decided to pull it out, possibly to mow the lawn there. But when I tugged I found it unyielding, so I got a stronger grip and yanked with all my might. Its stubbornness seemed to challenge me, and so I wrenched and struggled fiercely. In vain. I gave up. Suddenly there burst from beneath the bottom leaves a hen pheasant, despairingly flying off into the meadow. Stunned, I looked down to see a sedate bowl of tan eggs, which she had protected all through my thunderous thrashings. I stood there a long time marveling over the intensity of her motherly instinct, and the irony of my having threatened her and her treasure, in my ignorance of her presence. Both she and I had been attracted to this colorful focus on the grass—for her to hide, for me to pluck up. How intense for both of us! I often wondered, Did she ever come back? . . . Since then, the mullein has always seemed personal to me—whether I see it in Alsace or here along the Branch.

I am struck by the conflicted and powerful impulses in this story: the bird's to nest and the boy's to dislodge. Moreover, John follows the mullein's journey from Alsace, a European ancestral homeland, to his own birthplace along the northeast branch of the Perkiomen Creek in Pennsylvania, thereby linking a migratory plant with the migration of Anabaptist people. Because it is not native to North America, it is assumed that the mullein came here by ship, as the European immigrants did, imported as a useful herb.

Another old country plant is equally intriguing and associated with the mullein in my imagination. In the Netherlands, "Mennonite Sister" (*het menniste zusje*) is the common name of a plant that, though much smaller, is structured like the mullein with low-growing leaves and a single flowering spear. English versions of this plant's name are Pretty Nancy, Prattling Parnel, or Kiss Me Quick—all allusive to female allure, in keeping with the Dutch name. In his study of the Mennonite presence in seventeenth-century Dutch literature, Piet Visser reports that "Mennonite Sister" has been an idiomatic expression and idea in Dutch culture at least since 1621, when Jan Jansz Starter depicted her in a poem, and through the end of that century, when she appears in several popular dramas: a "prudish, shy, serious Mennonite girl" who is ultimately seduced by a non-Mennonite lover. This figure transgresses the bounds of her home community by associating with non-Mennonite suitors, as well as the community's, and perhaps her own, moral conventions.[8] She is a useful figure for a Mennonite woman in search of a literary precursor. Like Bertha, this mythic muse can legitimize a woman's desire to transcend social expectations, proving that there is more passion in a plain girl than meets the eye.

Promiscuous in her affections and allegiance, "Mennonite Sister" is an appropriate nickname for the plant *saxifraga umbrosa,* whose Latin name means "overshadowed stone-breaker." This name refers to the habits of a plant with roots that work their way into cracks on rocky banks, and it richly suggests that although the Mennonite sister may be "overshadowed" by her Mennonite brothers, she still manages to be a "stone-breaker"—a term not far from our idiom "ball breaker." Or, in keeping with the Dutch tradition, she is "overshadowed" by the foreign lover and undone by a desire that finally breaks through the stone of her own will and the community's strictures. This kind of liberty, it may be assumed, can lead only to the kind of transgression that causes her to abandon home and family. Yet with the help of the mullein, is it impossible to imagine her possessing roots *as well as* invisible wings, and to believe that her migrations may produce a healing tonic?

In American poetry, the saxifrage flower crops up in the final stanza of William Carlos Williams's poem "A Sort of a Song," which contains a statement of his own poetics. In this poem, Williams portrays the poet as a snake, waiting

Saxifrage, possibly *Saxifraga umbrosa.*

under a weed, "sharp/to strike, quiet to wait" (4–5), who seeks by way of metaphor to make peace between people and "the stones." The poet's art is a negotiation between the human and the inhuman, perhaps between the imperfect person and the stones of legalistic accusers. The final lines of the brief lyric articulate Williams's famous advice for modern American poets to become composers and innovators of a verse that is both delicate and powerful in its particularity:

> Compose. (No ideas
> but in things) Invent!
> Saxifrage is my flower that splits
> the rocks. (9–12)[9]

When I moved back to Pennsylvania to take a job at Messiah College, I had to obtain my first car at the age of thirty-three. With the blessing of both of my brothers, my father gave me Bertha's maroon 1978 Chevrolet Impala. Compared to most cars on the road, mine is an enormous rust boat, whose V-8 engine never runs more smoothly than when it is on the freeway, pushing the speed limit. Quite by accident, the license plate that came when we changed title on the car reads, "BAD-8460"—which I can only add to Bertha's alliterative list of dubious attributes: "bold, boisterous, bossy." Of course, the words *bomb* and *barge* also come to mind—as does the memory of the poet Amy Lowell. The great confessional poet Robert Lowell, a younger relative, described his mother's reaction to the famous female writer in their family: "Her poetry! But was *poetry* what one could call Amy's loud, bossy, unladylike *chinoiserie*—her free verse!" Robert's proper, class-conscious mother went on to characterize the early-twentieth-century traveler and poet—who, following the aesthetics of Chinese poetry, refused to follow the conventions of Western rhymed and metered verse—as one who "had the courage of her convictions," who "worked like a horse," and who "always did everything the *hard* way."[10]

Like stout Amy Lowell, my wide-sided car named Bertha is a reminder to speak up, to risk the transgressive gesture, and to put "the bite" and artful lye in whatever I write. If only in a symbolic sense, this car and these figures grant me a certain liberty and provide good company on the journey. They remind me that authority comes from the experience we gain by running off and talking with strangers; authority comes from dreams and fragments of memory and from tracking the ways of weeds, which thrive beyond the bounds of domestic gardens and gracefully bloom where no one ever planted them.

A final detail from my wildflower guide adds that in ancient Rome people dipped mullein stalks in oil to make torches and that the woolly leaves are still collected in some places for use as lamp wicking. Thus, through some miracle of human ingenuity, a migratory bloom can become a source of illumination. In a similar metaphoric vein, John Ruth recalls that his great-grandmother, Sarah Landis, dried mullein in her attic and, during the long winter months, smoked it in a pipe, pinching her nose shut and blowing through her ears, "to clear things up."

CAMP HILL, 1996

When the Stranger Is an Angel

3 Long ago, when my father was maybe three or four years old, before he'd gone to public school and learned to speak English, he met a hobo whom he remembers to this day. The man was one of the many homeless men who rode freight trains in search of work or adventure during the Depression, often depending upon the goodwill of strangers for food and lodging. Farms in the tiny, isolated valleys of central Pennsylvania were known among these men to be places where they could get a meal and sleep in a dry hayloft. During those years, many hobos passed though my father's Amish home, where a reverse-painting-on-glass motto in the living room reminded the family, "Be not forgetful to entertain strangers: for thereby some have entertained angels unawares" (Hebrews 13:2).

Of all the vagabonds who passed through, the one who stands out most in my father's memory was a bit dirty and tattered when he showed up after dinner time and well before supper that day. Although she was in the midst of canning cherries, my grandmother stopped to prepare a full meal for him, as was her custom—meat, potatoes, vegetables, bread, and a slice of pie. The man heaped his plate and walked out of the farmhouse, and the child who would become my father followed him to the porch steps where they sat down together. *"Wie bist du?"* (How are you?) the boy said softly at first, then again more loudly and slowly until he realized that he couldn't make the man understand that simple question. Nor could the boy understand the man's English reply. Content to watch him gobble his meal, the child fell silent, listening to the clink and scrape of silverware, breathing in bodily scents he had never smelled before: stale coffee and something strong like the liniment his mother rubbed on his chest when he fell ill with the grippe.

After he'd finished eating, the man carefully placed his dish and silverware aside on the porch boards and pulled a slender, sticklike object and a little box of matches from his pocket. He lit the cigarette and blew smoke from his nose while the boy watched, entirely engrossed. The man smiled and slowly stroked the boy's bowl-cut hair; then he reached into his trouser pocket and pulled out a watch tethered by a chain to his belt loop. The child bent over to watch the almost imperceptible progress of its minute hand. He turned the heavy, golden disk over in his palm and pressed his ear to the engraved scrolls and swirls. The soft ticking reminded him of the deep pulse of the mantle clock in the living room, which had intrigued him ever since he had seen his grandfather open a door on the back to reveal a mallet striking a thick wire coil.

At last the boy placed the watch back in the man's hand. He slipped it into a fold in his trousers, then pulled a photograph from his breast pocket and offered it to the child. The child studied the cracked studio portrait for a long time, holding it in both hands close to his face. He had not seen many images like this in his life. Looking up at the hobo, then back at the picture, he decided that the black-and-white photograph of a little boy with slicked hair must have depicted the man's grandson.

For many nights after that, when wind blew out of the southwest and the boy could hear train whistles from the other side of the mountain, he thought about that man and wondered about that little boy in the picture. It would be some years before he would get to see a train and many more before he would ride one, but he knew that those whistles and distant rumblings brought hobos to his farm and carried them away, as his mother explained. He tried to imagine where those men without families came from and where they went. Ever after that, he longed to cross the mountain and ride away on a freight train.

The first time I heard my father tell this story more than twenty years ago, I sensed that it held special significance, though I couldn't understand what it was, so I just remembered it. Like many of the stories from his childhood, it seemed to contain equal portions of sadness for the loss of his first culture and wonder at the pull of the wider world. It seemed to show that his decision to leave the community of his birth was almost inevitable: the child of his story is so young that he cannot stifle his curiosity or see the consequences of his own nature. Only later will he look back and realize that *that* is when he began to leave, without any knowledge of what he stood to lose or gain by doing so. Of all the stories he could select to explain his departure from his home culture, this appears among the most modest. In

The only photograph of my father during his childhood, taken by an uncle in the late 1930s, was rediscovered in recent years.

telling it, he seems to suggest that he left the Amish community, not to seek education or worldly opportunities, as it might appear to those who remained with the tradition, but only to satisfy his curiosity, aroused by an encounter with an ordinary hobo.

Some time ago, my father sent me a written version of this story, included in the text of a speech he had prepared for an audience of Mifflin County Lutherans who had invited him to speak about his experience of growing up in an Amish home. His interpretation of the story surprised me, since I'd always seen it as a powerful lesson about individuals, not community. Yet he told this story to illustrate the type of hospitality that Amish folk offer to anyone who drops in unannounced—*Freundschaft* (kin), friend, or stranger—an ethic he admires very much. "Hospitality" was one of three points that he celebrated in his talk entitled "Amish Spiritual Heritage"; the other two points were "Silence" and "the Joy of Work."

The more I consider this story, the more complex and indeterminate its meaning becomes, wandering farther and farther from whatever I imagine my father now believes it must mean. As an illustration of hospitality, the story contains only one stranger, the hobo. But I see in this story at least two strangers—maybe three, if you count me. When I was young, I longed to be like my father, whose job as a medical researcher caused him to travel to distant cities, while our mother stayed home with us children. I recall once hearing him describe a night when he rode public bus lines all over a western city rather than sleep, just to see what was there. When our family moved from a farm to the edge of a village in western Pennsylvania, I used to wander off habitually, unable to observe the boundaries of town-sized lawns; more than once my distraught mother found her three- or four-year-old daughter talking with neighbors or just walking along the road. She scolded and punished, even raised the specter of the Lindbergh baby kidnapping, but I remained heedless of her warnings. Later, as my younger brother and I walked to grade school, daily crossing a skeletal wooden railroad overpass blackened with oil and soot, I'd tell him that one morning we would bring our pillows along, tie them to our butts with belts, jump down onto the open coal cars, and ride the mainline of the Pennsylvania Central to Pittsburgh or Chicago.

As I understand it, my father's story is not so much about the hobo as it is a story of how the boy became a stranger. As long as I can see him sitting out there on the porch long before I was born, taking in the strong breath of a stranger, I don't feel so alone listening to other strangers, caught among communities in the transitional space that has become my home. My need for this story and my understanding of it have changed its telling in many ways. When my father tells it, he supplies fewer details: his mother is only working when the hobo shows up; we don't know what she is doing. There is no mantle clock to suggest inevitable passings or to link the stranger's watch with the boy's experience. There is the smell of that so-called liniment, but no grippe. According to my father, there was more than one memorable hobo in his childhood; one had the watch, and another the photograph.

The version I tell reflects my intention to concentrate the power of the story, and it reveals my conflicting desires to at once expose and protect the community. While I seek to discover new meanings, I am ashamed to tell what I already understand. I call the stranger a hobo, for instance, but my father called him a "bum," that community's term for drifters who were unconnected to family or community and who seemed unable or unwilling to do honest work. *Hobo*, the word I chose, was first coined from the blending of the words *homeward* and *bound*, a name given to the Union soldiers walking back to their towns and cities in the north after the Civil War. Thus, embedded in that word is the suggestion that a home awaits even the drifter at the end of his journey—but this may be only my fancy.

For each of the details in my version of the story that do not match my father's, others remain stable, critical to its substance. In addition to the boy and the stranger, the story retains the cigarette, pocket watch, photograph, and porch. These persist, first in my father's mind, then in my own, because they serve as emblems of individuality and worldliness. A manufactured cigarette is alien in a culture of ascetic

HOW MY FATHER
LEARNED ENGLISH

Breathing his own breath,
forehead pressed in a corner
while the teacher's syllables
pelted his back, meaningless.
At some point, he says, it just
began to make sense, sounds gave
up significance as neatly
as the clear and yolk slipped
into batter when his mother tapped
a bowl and pulled egg shells apart.
How could she bear to think

of her first-grader, mute and confused
the long season from Labor Day
to Christmas, begging translation
from desk mates, pestering hired men
for names of things during chores?
She knew he'd eventually piece together
a tongue with words from home
and school. Only this fall I think
to ask how that happened, though
I've taught English for years,
eagerly asking the foreigners
to tell me about their homes,
Please, I urge, say it in English.

farmers; like coffee and alcohol, it is costly, sensuous, completely useless, even dangerous. It is foreign and carnal, and its menace is connected with an actual, all-consuming threat. How could a farmer trust strangers with fire in the haymow? My father says that grandpa walked the hobos to the barn in the evening, forked together a hay bed for them, then confiscated their cigarettes and matches. Occasionally he trusted someone enough to let him keep them, probably after an evening of lively conversation around the kitchen table with the stranger and my grandmother.

The pocket watch is an aesthetic object of artifice, a mechanical representation of the passage of time, which human beings first experience in the natural cycles associated with season and sun—creation, that is, with God. Gold and engraved, it is more ornate than the wooden mantle clocks common to Amish living rooms, and it exists purely for the use and pleasure of an individual rather than for the functioning of an entire family. The photograph is also an object of artifice, produced by a technology forbidden in a culture that values the authentic, the human, and the traditional.

Gazing intently upon the photograph, the child of my imagination was able to read the picture like a text. In his written version of the story, my father says that he assumed the boy in the picture was the hobo's grandson. I can imagine my father as a child constructing a narrative there on the porch: the boy in the picture must love this hobo, as my father loves his grandfathers Spicher and Yoder. But the hobo left him; now the hobo misses that boy, and the boy misses him as my father would miss his own grandfathers. Perhaps my father sensed a personal connection with the boy in the picture; perhaps he reminded the stranger of a faraway grandson. Maybe the boy in the picture was the hobo himself, once upon a time. Or perhaps my father was like the boy in some other way: the photograph frames an individual figure, a child alone, isolated from even his own family.

In my father's story, he doesn't explain why he and the hobo sat out on the porch. Yet I know that Amish and Mennonite families often required hobos and traveling peddlers to dine outdoors, just as they required them to sleep in the barn. Neither inside nor outside the house, the porch served as a safety zone for a community afraid of physical infection from strangers. Regarding the men as unclean and fearing tuberculosis—which my Amish grandmother later contracted—Mennonite and Amish women boiled dishes and silverware after a hobo finished eating. Some may even have feared spiritual infection. I am told that some of the more evangelical-minded Mennonites sent the hobos off the next morning with Bible tracts in hand. Before his death, Warren Rohrer, who grew up in Lancaster County, told me that he once found a great cache of those tracts, weathered and fading, in a ravine on his family's farm. Still a boy then, he was intrigued by the idea that the hobos all seemed to know exactly where to unload those spiritual messages before leaving his family's property. It was as though they understood the limits of cultural and spiritual boundaries and knew how far a bounded salvation could travel from its source.

For my father, the porch was not a safety zone but a transitional space where he could sit with the stranger and begin to imagine his transient way of life. The child did not maintain that formal sense of

THE ONLY PHOTOGRAPH OF MY FATHER AS A BOY

In Amish trousers and suspenders,
he's barefoot by the field lane,
blond hair bowl-cut, his face twisted.
He knows this shouldn't be—
this worldly uncle squinting into a box
camera, commanding, "Hold still."
That click, something flew out of him
with, "Don't tell your mother 'bout this."
And something flew in. The next picture,
high school graduation, he's grinning
on the rim of the world,
as confident as science in 1951.

hospitality that is quite compatible with preserving the boundaries of a closed community. Instead, he left his mother in the kitchen and went out to be with the hobo. He held out his small hands and allowed the hobo to place into them his most precious personal possessions. In a gesture that is similar to what happens when we share the essential stories of our lives with others, the hobo invited the boy to consider what was most important to him, to gaze upon what he loved. Thus, by his example, the hobo taught the child how to treat strangers, showing a generosity and sharing of self that may have been unlike the charity offered mostly out of obedience to a Bible verse.

That form of obligatory hospitality seems to be related to the idea of "hospital"—a place where services are rendered efficiently by professional caretakers but where the stories of the ill are rarely attended to. In spite of all of their goodwill, nurses and doctors can rarely come to know the souls connected to the bodies of the strangers they heal, and they rarely have time to be changed by their encounters with them. This attitude toward others reminds me of a character in Zora Neale Hurston's novel, *Their Eyes Were Watching God*. Joe Starks, the proud benefactor of a new all-Negro town, is described by a member of his community as "uh man dat changes everything, but nothin' don't change him."[1] To help others but to remain unmoved by encounters with them is a kind of hubris and a failure to be open to the transforming power of human relationship.

I believe that my father started to become a stranger the day he met that hobo, assuming that the distinguishing mark of the stranger is his uncanny ability to call into question the norms and certainties of the community he inhabits. As I tell the story, the child was profoundly changed by this encounter with the stranger. Because he was able to imagine the hobo's life as something entirely different from anything he'd experienced in his own community, my father grew into a young man whose increasingly insistent questions would cause him to seek answers in the wider world. Destined to leave the community of his birth, he would also exist slightly outside the history, language, customs, and traditions of the places he would inhabit thereafter. Only vaguely conscious of missed allusions and gaps in common knowledge, he would, for instance, astound his own children with his inability to identify characters in the most common fairy tales. Because he would always carry the perspective of another place, he would challenge the conventions of the communities that would adopt him even as he learned how to belong to them.[2]

In an event that mirrors the hobo's generosity on the porch, that child would go on to describe to his Lutheran neighbors his sense of loss and the values from his home that he cherished most. And whether he intended to or not, he would also pass this story like a precious legacy into the hands of at least one of his children. For me, the story is useful in understanding my position between the community of family and home, and the communities I now inhabit. I cannot tell where I am in the story's terms—whether my choice to move to a city and pursue a life of writing and dialogue with strangers means that I'll end up sleeping in the barn, or whether an empty bed waits upstairs in the farmhouse for me, or whether I'll even want a place there some day. I suspect that I may finally sleep outside the constructs of this story altogether. Meanwhile, it serves to link my experience with my father's, an important validation of porch-sitting and decisions made before I knew exactly where listening to strangers might lead.

In the end, I wonder if the hobo in this story was not the angel promised by the Bible verse in my father's boyhood living room. For what is an angel but a stranger who is an agent of transformation? Consider Jacob that night on his way to make reparations with his estranged brother, Esau. According to the text, he first separated his family from the large band of servants and livestock, setting up a small camp for them some distance away. Jacob then ventured farther into the night, toward his past and family of origin. Separated from his immediate family's campfire, alone, he met a man who refused to say his own name. After hours of intense engagement with this stranger, Jacob was so transformed that the stranger gave him a new name.

According to tradition, Jacob became the great leader called Israel because his wrestling partner that night was an angel. But could it not also be true that the stranger became an angel *because* Jacob allowed himself to be touched and transformed, even crippled and renamed, through the encounter? Perhaps this story—like my father's story—means that we possess a sacred power to make angels out of strangers when we are open to change. This can only happen when we leave the security of the hearth and go out to greet the stranger, when we sit with him and imagine his life, when we are able to question our certainties and to be taught and changed through the encounter.

BROOKLYN, 1993

WRITING HOME

Bringing Home the Work

4 Shortly after I learned that *Sleeping Preacher* had found a publisher, I began to get migraine headaches, more in one week than I had usually gotten in a whole year. It didn't take much for me to realize that they were related to the prospect of publication, especially to the fear of my work being read by my family and the Mennonite relatives about whom I'd written.

My older brother once observed, "You publish your work, but never bring it home to us—strangers know you better than we do." It's true. All those years I'd been scribbling away, keeping my thoughts more or less to myself, sharing the poems with other students or poets, and occasionally publishing in little magazines read mostly by writers and professors.

A book is more public and permanent though—never mind the fact that it was selected by the University of Pittsburgh Press, located not thirty miles from my parents' house. No longer able to hide the work from my family, I realized that I really didn't want to, since in some respects they represented its primary audience. Many of the poems are based on family stories and memory, examining the particular history of our extended clan and its Mennonite and Amish community. So I sent copies of the manuscript home and waited for the calls, gripped by a kind of fear I'd rarely experienced in almost a decade of living in New York City. All the while, I wondered where that fear comes from and whether those of us who try to write from our experiences in traditional, closed communities are especially prone to it.

When I described my anxiety to Patrick Friesen, a Canadian poet of Mennonite ethnicity, he wrote back sensibly, "Goes with the territory, doesn't it?" In Canada, where enough notable fiction writers and poets have emerged in the past forty years to constitute the beginnings of a Mennonite tradition, it does go with the territory. Critic and editor Hildi Froese Tiessen clearly described this phenomenon in the introduction to *Liars and Rascals,* her collection of short fiction by thirteen contemporary Canadians of Mennonite background. The title she chose refers, not to the stories, but to the authors and their uneasy relations with Mennonite readers, and she describes its sources in her introduction.

The rascal is novelist Rudy Wiebe, who, upon the publication of his 1962 novel *Peace Shall Destroy Many,* left his job as editor of a church magazine and the Mennonite community of Winnipeg in the midst of controversy. With Hildi, Rudy visited the Mennonite Museum in Steinback, Manitoba, some twenty years later. There they met a soft-spoken museum employee who, upon hearing Rudy's name, exclaimed in Low German, "Not the rascal!" Rudy shrugged and suggested that perhaps the man was thinking of someone else.

The liar is Jacob Janzen, a Mennonite playwright and novelist who emigrated from Russia to Canada in 1924. In a 1946 essay, he told this story:

> When I came to Canada and in my broken English tried to make plain to a Mennonite bishop that I was a "novelist" (that being the translation for *Schriftsteller* in my dictionary), he was much surprised. He then tried to make plain to me that "novelists" were fiction writers and that fiction was

a lie. I surely would not want to represent myself to him as a professional liar. . . . I admitted to myself, but not aloud to him, that I was just that kind of "liar" which had caused him such a shock.[1]

It was the "lies" in my own work that prompted my mother to call and report the inaccuracies that she'd circled throughout my manuscript. My great-aunt's car was a Chevy, not a Buick, as I'd written, for instance. She knows that poetry isn't journalism, yet she had to express her discomfort with the blend of fact and fiction that often generates imaginative writing. It's true that Mennonites have not been in the habit of changing details to suit the story: from our very first confessions of faith we've expected language to be a useful, solid bucket to hold truths as clear as water. Writers and scholars, on the other hand, play with language, realizing the rich possibilities of a convention that is full of holes and gaps in meaning. (Of course, when a bucket springs a leak, you insist on mending it if you're Mennonite; only troublemakers go around poking at holes.)

In other places in the manuscript, my mother agreed that the story was correct, but she wondered if I couldn't find kinder words to express my meaning. Her concern seemed to spring from that long tradition that has asked us, especially us women, to soften our language or to remain silent: "If you don't have anything nice to say . . . " No doubt she was considering the feelings of the only other people who would know whether the stories had been stretched. And those relatives probably would not be as offended by the misnaming of a car as they might be by other larger issues. Maybe she was wondering how she would bridge the distance between the community and her daughter when the book finally appeared. I hung up the phone, wondering why she had not focused on any of the book's central themes, those tensions common to much contemporary Mennonite writing and central to my life: individual/community, outside/inside, city/country, profane/sacred, female/male.

Her defensive reading strategy, I realized, almost parallels the way I created many of the poems in the first place. For instance, one of the longer pieces in the collection, titled "Mennonites," was written quickly when I was feeling particularly estranged from my secular, urban environment, as some sort of attempt to explain what a Mennonite is. When I showed the piece to a friend, she said, "Wow. There's a lot of anger here." I was surprised to see it but glad that a temporary blindness had enabled me to get the poem down before I could censor myself. Readers can be as blind as writers in this way, deflecting meanings that conflict with the expectations they bring to the text. So then I wonder if I've unconsciously written a book that is unreadable to the members of the community about whom it was written. Or is it only that every child's text resists the readings of her parents?

Certainly many other writers have had difficulty with the folks back home, Thomas Wolfe with his *You Can't Go Home Again* among them. In October 1991, around the time I was having headaches, South African novelist Nadine Gordimer won the Nobel Prize for literature and was quoted on the front page of the *New York Times*: "The best way to be read is posthumously. That way it doesn't matter if you offend a friend or a relative or a lover."[2] But for a Mennonite writer, the situation seems much more intense; the Mennonite community can be equivalent to friend, relative, lover, and enemy all rolled into one.

Studio portrait of my mother and me taken in the mid-1960s.

Poet Di Brandt, who grew up in a Mennonite farm village in Manitoba, told me some time ago that she feared she would be "hounded out of the community" if her work were ever to appear in print. She published her first book only after it had been repeatedly solicited for two years, and then she took it back once in a loss of nerve. When it finally did appear, she had to face an angry crowd back home. "It was very traumatic for my mother—this book," Di recalled. "People have asked her, 'Do you still love your daughter?' It was hard because she didn't know what to say about it. She didn't understand really why I wrote it and didn't know how to defend it. So she had to learn how to defend me."

Perhaps for Di, and certainly for me, the fear of publishing a first book is a fear of conflict that reaches well beyond the typical writerly anxieties of self-revelation and failure to meet literary standards. That kind of dread is familiar to the Swiss-Pennsylvania Amish and Mennonites of my background, who silenced errant preachers to check their authority. It is essentially a fear of abandonment and dislocation that reaches back to the time when an outspoken dissenter—whether she was forced to leave or to conform to the community's will—lost dearly, either in terms of her context in the world or in terms of her own voice. Shunning means censorship, and self-censorship is also excommunication.

Attuned to the dangers that go with violating community standards, my father said, after reading my manuscript, "I think you should consider the fact that if you publish a book with the 'f-word' in it, you might never get a job at a Mennonite college." Whether or not that is so, he sensed that a transgression in language might jeopardize my status in the community. A man whose days began in an Amish home and ended in a large corporation, he knows what it means to burn bridges in one's youth and how, when rebuilt from the other side, they can never be crossed in the same way.

To return to the community of my memory by way of writing is to return as a stranger. The work of poetry requires that a person gain deep access to her emotional life and write to make sense of it. To do

EVE'S CURSE

To the beautiful student, as her blue eyes glaze
and brighten in their brine, I cannot say,
Yes, it will be as you suspect. This work
will drive you away from us; it will make
you strange in the end. Though you were raised
in Pennsylvania, the state which retains
more of its natives than any other,
the only state that contains all the letters
you need to write "live," you will leave.
Because these sweet limestone fields sustained
you and all of us before this, your curse
will be to ache as you've never imagined:
your limbs will long for the scent of this ridge,
as Eve's curse was to crave for her husband.

this she must assume a certain authority, a belief that her perceptions are true and worth telling. Yet to brood over one's existence and to speak in this way is antithetical to the long tradition of *Demut* (humility) and *Gelassenheit* (submission) so embedded in many Mennonite souls. Moreover, such activity lacks an apparent usefulness in the material world. To grow up as the kind of Mennonite I was and to write poetry that probes the reality of that experience is a serious contradiction. (A reflective essay like this also borders on embarrassing that sensibility.)

Nonetheless, I believe that the making of written texts is a calling of high seriousness, and I feel indebted to my background for my sense of this value. Over the years, however, I've struggled to rely less and less on given meanings, and instead, to construct individual ones from my own experience: to make art. Tension, for both writers and readers, arises when the individual meanings collide with the received meanings endorsed by the community.

In a review of *Liars and Rascals* that appeared in the weekly Canadian newspaper, the *Mennonite Reporter,* John Ruth—who years later would be nicknamed by my husband "John Truth"—clearly expressed this tension. While he said many positive things about the artistic quality of the collection, his main complaint was that "the big Truth is here by implications, while little truths have the stage." He had read the book searching for a single expression of the "communal soul" that would somehow offer a standard interpretation of the collective experience, but whatever message he found was faint and ambiguous. Instead, he complained, the collection was dominated by "individual psyches offended by a stingy heritage."[3]

Perhaps John would count me among the offended, for I think that there is something very stingy about a heritage that has handed us a way of reading that puts such strenuous demands on readers and writing and, by extension, on writers. I think that Mennonites approach literature from a Platonic perspective, as transmitted through Western Christianity, measuring texts against a set hierarchy. On the top are the Bible, followed by the *Martyrs Mirror* and other writings that point directly to the higher Truth. Below this are the serious forms that enlighten for the right objectives. (This must be where John wanted the *Liars and Rascals* stories to land.) Last is the literature that may only amuse—or even corrupt—and that should be avoided by serious people altogether.

It is interesting to note that, when Mennonite editor and writer Levi Miller reviewed *Liars and Rascals,* he also referred to a hierarchy of reading: "On one level, these stories give authentic voice to this yielded (*Gelassenheit*) Christian community. . . . On another level, many of these stories are simply a good read."[4] Perhaps since publishing his novel, *Ben's Wayne,* and returning to the Ohio Amish community of its origin, Levi understands the consequences of judging a book by Platonic standards. Still, he divides the "authentic" voice of the community from the individualistic pleasure of reading and places them on different levels. He appreciates stories that speak in an accent both strikingly familiar and strangely alien because the voices of his community come to him in another form, on the printed page. Mennonite stories, after all, echo individual Mennonite experiences in a way that other kinds of mainstream fiction may not; they have the power to tempt us to remember and to reconsider our particular experience in new ways.

It is a weird and frightful season, the time between the promise and date of publication—long enough to imagine the book in another's hands, to anticipate responses from readers like Levi and John and my great-aunts. It is a time to come to terms with what it means to print one's story. For me that has meant facing what I've known all along: that when a writer attempts to render a common experience without mouthing the common beliefs, conflict is imminent. Before publication, the story exists only in the space of its oral telling or in its standard versions. When it appears on paper, roughened by an individual consciousness, it lies vulnerable to all the expectations of accuracy and ultimacy that Mennonites bring to a text. These are my doubts: What if you read my book and tell me that I've got it all wrong, that my perceptions have no relation to a reality shaped by our collective experience? What if you call me a liar and cast me out?

Paradoxically, a precarious sense of location is exactly what has fueled much of my writing so far. Many of the poems in *Sleeping Preacher* were written from the perspective of an outsider—either a Mennonite outside American culture or a critical sheep in the Mennonite fold. I've had it both ways—to be in the community and in the world—which of course means to have it neither way. Alienating as it sometimes feels, this non-home is my home, and on a good day I count a sense of disequilibrium among my greatest gifts.

Some of my thirty-something urban friends from traditional Mennonite homes are working hard to get over whatever sets them apart from the mainstream, feeling that the conflict between a Mennonite past and their present lives is best resolved in the privacy of a psychotherapist's office. At times I almost feel this way too. Perhaps if I write enough Mennonite poems, I will one day break through this invisible sphere that both comforts and confines and at last be released into . . . what? The world, whatever that means? A clean, blank space free of our inescapable history?

BROOKLYN, 1991

Preacher's Striptease

5

When *Sleeping Preacher* was being prepared for publication, some at the press raised concerns about the name I'd chosen for the book. They suggested that I use the more accessible, more marketable title of one of the poems in the collection, "Mennonites." I resisted this idea. It was a fearful enough thing to publish work about my Amish and Mennonite background without giving the book a name that suggested I claimed to represent the entire tribe. Although I was, and continue to be, very grateful to my editor, I did not change the title. Instead, my husband, David—who has never been comfortable referring to his Mennonite Brethren heritage in his work—said, "Don't worry. I'll make a picture that shouts 'Mennonite.'" For the cover, he painted his only piece of obviously ethnic art to date, a faux primitive that contains every popular Amish signifier he could think of: quilt, horse and buggy, conspicuous traditional plain dress, rural landscape, and rustic furniture. From his perspective, the image is ironic or even a little campy, but I know that most viewers do not see this. In fact, I've met readers

David Kasdorf. *Sleeping Preacher.*

who tell me they discovered my work because they were drawn to the book's beautiful cover.

For many, the pleasing pink image promises something that the book seems to deliver: like the rectangle above the bed, the poems are understood to be either a window through which to view a fascinating subculture or an artful representation of that subculture, like a painting or photograph. Reviews repeatedly expressed this sense: an unidentified reviewer in *Publisher's Weekly* said, "The material presents an interesting and unusually close portrait of the Amish people"; Emily Grosholz of *The Hudson Review* said, "The interest of *Sleeping Preacher* . . . lies in its depiction of Amish society."[1] Both "depict" and "portrait" suggest visual renderings of the subject, a written vision of a society that is generally hidden from view. Characterized by plain-spoken family stories and imagistic realism, the book continues to be used as a classroom text at both religious and secular colleges for undergraduate courses with titles like "Writing about America" to represent what may be our nation's favorite minority group. The Amish are people who are typically understood to be peaceable and not associated with criminal activity, hardworking and neither dependent on public assistance nor eager to enter competitive, professional job markets, nonlitigious and unlikely to challenge what others say about them, and evidently of European descent—all in all, safe subjects in a multicultural society.

Thus, after having passed myself off as a regular white girl at New York University for nearly a decade, I became an ethnic author in 1991. In the years since then, I've had time to consider the expectations of authenticity, the responsibility of representation, and the questions of my reading audience—or rather, audiences. Whether I am explaining to a relative why a poem doesn't report the facts as he recalls them or trying to counteract the ethnic generalizations in a National Public Radio interview, I have been unable to avoid situations in which I must account for myself and my work. Over the years, I have found some useful ways of thinking about these things through the example and vocabulary of postcolonial and women writers, especially those of color. Trying to gather my thoughts along these lines, my mind returns to the painting that David made out of spite and love for my first book. I see in it a structure for a meditation on two audiences and two traditions as well as on the ways that writing in a second genre—the essay—has enabled me to describe, and perhaps even escape, my position between them.

The painting contains three main elements that form a triangle when a viewer's eye travels between them: the window or picture which, for the purposes of this essay, I will take to represent the actual Amish tradition and traditional community (or what viewers imagine it to be); the chair with an overturned book on it, which I take to represent the literary tradition and contemporary literary community; and the brown-haired female in bed, who lies parallel to and just above my name on the book cover, a representation of myself, or at least myself in the author's position. The visual center of the painting is the quilt, prized souvenir of visits to Amish country, a material expression of a nonmaterialistic culture that can be purchased and taken home.

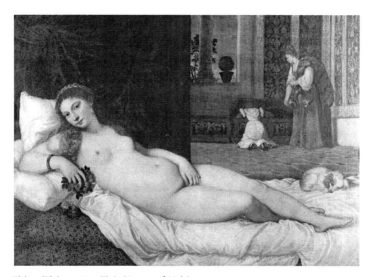

Titian (Tiziano Vecellio). *Venus of Urbino.*

Pull the quilt off the cover of *Sleeping Preacher,* and this painting is a pastiche of traditional nudes, such as Titian's *Venus.* In these pictures, the female body is artfully arranged for the pleasure of the spectator beyond the picture plane—her lovely face meets our gaze serenely; breast and thigh tilt toward us—so that the collector who owns the painting also possesses the body of a lovely woman. Pull the plain dress off of an Amish or Mennonite person, and there is only a human body; behind the veil of my ethnic identity articulated in *Sleeping Preacher* is only a woman. Perhaps it is no surprise that a second book of poems, which has fewer explicit references to my background, is called *Eve's Striptease.* As a follow-up to *Sleeping Preacher,* this title also troubled my editor, who wondered whether it was too commercial and provocative. Once again, however, he complied with my wishes. On the cover of the second book, a friend's photograph shows an undershirt flying in the wind; the female body is absent, suggested only by implication of the gesture that tossed her own shirt.

When he made the cover painting for *Sleeping Preacher,* David says, he hadn't seen *La Bacchante* by Félix Trutat, which he discovered later, leafing through John Berger's little book, *Ways of Seeing.* It is uncanny that the two pictures, created more than one hundred years apart, are iconographically identical: a classic nude composition complicated with the insertion of a male spectator peering through a window above an unsuspecting female's bed. The male spectator in both of these pictures refers to the idea of seeing and reminds viewers that we are also spectators. That dynamic is further compounded in David's painting because the male spectator within the frame seems to belong to the world of the woman's ethnic community, whereas viewers outside the frame are likely to be part of broader American society. Seen in this way, the painting connotes a kind of double spectatorship: ethnic male views ethnic female, while nonethnic viewers see them both. There is likewise double desire: for the female in the classic nude pose and for the ethnic world depicted as a lost golden age when people lived at a slower pace, in harmony with family, nature, and God—represented in David's painting by the apparently pacific relations across gender and generation in this plain context.

Writing of sight and perception during the 1970s, Berger made

Carol Shadford. *Striptease.*

Félix Trutat. *La Bacchante.*

much of a notion that has since become commonplace in feminist discourse—that the female consciousness is divided, embodying both sight and spectator. She sees from both within herself and slightly outside herself, constantly watching to determine whether she meets the expectations of masculine desire, having internalized his ideal image of beauty and femininity.[2] Similarly, minority people may internalize both negative and positive stereotypes that broader society projects upon them and then measure themselves against them. As W. E. B. DuBois observed of African-American consciousness at the turn of the nineteenth century, "It is a peculiar sensation, this double consciousness, this sense of always looking at one's self through the eyes of others, of measuring one's soul by the tape of a world that looks on in amused contempt and pity."[3] To sustain one's sense of self despite this divided consciousness must take a great deal of energy.

As a Mennonite author, I have become both spectator and sight, conscious of conventional expectations about my background and the ways that my work fulfills or fails to meet those expectations. It troubles me that I used to tell a plainer story of my writing life for rea-

HOW TO WRITE
THE NEW MENNONITE POEM
Jeff Gundy

Choose two from old Bibles, humbly
    beautiful quilts,
Fraktur, and the *Martyrs Mirror* in Dutch.
Get the word "Mennonite" in at least
twice, once in the title, along with zwieback,
vareniki, borscht, and the farm,
which if possible should be lost now.

Grandmothers are very good, especially
dead grandmothers, especially speaking
German in Russia. They should have
Suffered. Mothers are good and may
have Quirks, if lovable. Male ancestors
are possible but presumed to represent
the patriarchy and to have abused

"their" wives, children, farm animals;
steer clear unless you are Angry,
or can supply affidavits from
everybody who knew them.

It is important to acknowledge
the spiritual and reproductive
superiority of plain coats and
coverings, the marvelous integrity
of those uncorrupted by television
and Mennonite higher education.
Use quaintness, brisk common sense
and a dash of barnyard humor to show
that they are Just Folks Too.

Remember that while the only good Mennonite
is not a dead Mennonite, many dead
Mennonites were really good. Work in
two or three. Dirk Willems

sons of convenience, self-preservation, and courtesy. That story was largely the American immigrant's story told in *Sleeping Preacher*: journey from (old) country to city, from tradition and innocence to experience. Even so, I was conscious of my own contradictions and complex reflexivity; I knew that my path was not that straightforward, nor was my attitude toward my past as unclouded and generous as the ideal Mennonite's should be.

Poet and Mennonite college professor Jeff Gundy has captured this kind of double-consciousness in a spoof that expresses its central tensions. His poem pokes fun at the overly self-conscious "new Mennonite" poet who has internalized society's desire for cultural stereotypes and who clutters his poems with signs of authenticity: ethnic food and European ancestors, the memory of martyrdom, plain dress, and

is hot this year. Include a woman,
an African if you know any, and
a Methodist with redeeming qualities.

You, of course, are a backslidden,
overlearned, doubtridden, egodriven
quasibeliever who would be less anxious
and surer of salvation if you could
only manage to give up the car,
the CD player, and coaching soccer.
You really want to be like Grandma.
You believe in discipleship, granola,
and the Peace Tax Fund, but things are
Complicated. You think about them plenty.
You plan to give up something, soon.

If you're in a major city, which
you should be, say something about
the streets, how you really hate
the place but get all charged up

walking around on your days off
looking at stuff and drinking
exotic coffee. Mention that this
seems strange to you, as does
the fact that sometimes you like sex,
even when you know the people in
the next apartment are listening.
Put your wedding ring in the poem
to reassure your parents.

Use the laser printer, and send
a large, glossy, black and white
photograph, just in case. Wear
something simple and dark. Smile
but not too hard. Let your eyes
reflect the miles you have come,
the centuries, your gratitude, your guilt.[4]

rural farm life. At the same time, the writer projects the correct Mennonite attitude that is a combination of humility and respect for one's tradition. The irony in this poem draws on the speaker's awareness that he is both sight and spectator.

This poem was written in 1993 as Gundy was beginning to glimpse the possibility of a Mennonite literary culture south of the Canadian border, and it was written partly in response to the attention granted to the "new Mennonite" poetry in *Sleeping Preacher,* which appeared late in 1992. Elsewhere Gundy has argued that no singular Mennonite community or identity is portrayed in current Mennonite poetry.[5] Here he manages to capture the "complicated"—and slightly neurotic—ways of a representative urban Mennonite character who enacts the prevailing cultural stereotypes. His group resists learning, stresses simplicity of lifestyle, and values humility and self-sacrificial deeds as the ultimate expression of piety. In the final strophe, the poet has the ambition of any writer, but a good Mennonite would never be that overt about it. So he performs in compliance with the expected norm, wears "something simple and dark," and affects an expression of gratitude for his heritage that is sufficiently tinged with guilt for having betrayed it. Writing poetry, owning a car or CD player, living in a city, or liking sex—nearly any pleasurable aspect of life—is a betrayal of the stern tradition (or at least a betrayal of whatever people imagine Mennonite tradition to be). Thus Gundy humorously details the internal conflicts of the "new Mennonite" poet caught between the expectations of the traditional community and the demands of his literary career.

The tension between the religious community and literary culture is also subtly illustrated by the tight triangle in David's painting. All three of those points—ethnic community with its rich oral tradition, literary community with its powerful textual tradition, and my writerly desire—were essential in creating the poem and, indeed, the entire book that bears its image. Furthermore, I think that something about the nature of the relationships between these elements becomes clear when a simple question is asked of each point on the triangle: What do you see?

Book

What does the book see? It sees the window and the girl. If they are viewed in relationship, the literary world understands that this author's work draws on memory and oral tradition. The perception most often expressed in reviews of *Sleeping Preacher* is that the value of my book lies in its subject matter and its ability to represent another group. Even before the book appeared, the poem "Mennonites" was included in a multicultural reader titled *The Many Worlds of Literature,* edited by Rutgers University professor Stuart Hirschberg and published by Macmillan. The cover of this textbook, a gorgeous aerial view of the earth overlaid with small photographs of assorted dark-skinned people in exotic costumes, reminds my friend

Crystal of the missionary literature from her fundamentalist Christian childhood. And there is something vaguely imperialistic about an index organized by continent and nation. While these categories appear to be straightforward for everywhere else on earth, the United States is divided into numerous subcategories that refer to race, ethnicity, and even religion. The difficulty of sorting people in this way becomes immediately apparent when one considers the identities of the authors listed above the subcategories—those presumed to be regular Americans. Among them is Adrienne Rich, who, by her own account in the essay "Split at the Root," fits into at least four minority categories she can name—Jew, lesbian, Southern, woman. Mine is the only name listed under "Mennonite," just above "Mohawk." And the poem "Mennonites" appears beneath a biographical blurb wildly embellished from the contributor's note in *Looking for Home: Women Writing About Exile,* an anthology where the poem previously appeared and presumably where Professor Hirschberg found it: "Julia Kasdorf grew up in a Mennonite community in Pennsylvania and is now a community activist working with local immigrant associations in Brooklyn."[6] I have never worked as an activist or with immigrants in Brooklyn, but perhaps that seems a likely enough vocation for the Mennonite type portrayed in the poem. In this biographical note, I am wrapped in a quilt, the contours of my actual life masked by expectations of ethnicity.

But if poems are reduced to being only clues to cultural identity, this is an easy enough mistake to make. Whereas the heady days of 1970s feminism put us in the habit of reading poems merely as expressions of personal experience, 1980s multiculturalism seems to have led us to read poetry only as a representation of community experience. Jan Montefiore has demonstrated that a limiting and unrecognized Romanticism informs the basic assumptions behind earlier feminist poetics: the idea that poetry articulates personal experience and that the poet is a transcendent representative of humanity, her work springing from memory and feeling.[7]

When I claim to write in plain speech the stories of my memory, I

THINKING OF CERTAIN MENNONITE WOMEN

When I think I can't bear to trace
one more sorrow back to its source,

I think of Lois those summer evenings,
when, supper dishes done, she'd climb

a windmill and cling beneath its great blades
drawing water from under her father's fields.

She'd stay there until the sun went down
on barn roof, garden, and the one paved road

pointing toward town. When I am afraid
to set out once more alone, I see Julie

pumping her legs so hard, she believes
she will fly off the swing set and land

gently on the lawn. I see her let go,
braids streaking behind, then see her knees

am an inheritor and practitioner of this poetic, as flawed and overly simple as I now find it to be. Moreover, for an ethnic poet, the individualistic Wordsworthian ideal expands to impossible proportions because it implies that an author can somehow channel the voice of an entire community—as if a community could be single-voiced, as if that sleeping girl in the painting can see more than whatever lies just outside her window. In *Many Worlds of Literature,* this expectation is clearly articulated in "Questions for Discussion and Writing," which direct student readers to listen to "Mennonites" as if they were "eaves-drop[ping]" and "directly hearing the inner voice of the community."[8] However seductive, this notion is mistaken because it assumes both too

shredded on gravel, stuck to stockings
each time she kneels to pray at a pew.

When I can't tell my own desire
from the wishes of others, I remember

my mom, too young to know or care better,
flinging her jumper, blouse, socks and slip

into the wind, dancing for flower beds
until her mother finds her. When I wonder

how I should live this only one life,
I think of how they tell these stories:

honestly, without explanation,
to whoever will listen.

much and also too little about the work of the imagination and how
poems actually come to be.

If not in drafting, then certainly in revision, I often consider tension, irony, precision, and ambiguity, to name only a few of the favored
Modernist touchstones. As a reader of my own work, I feel most the
strain of contradiction in "Mennonites," where people strive for perfection to the point of tidying up after God, insisting on a will to love
even in the face of physical harm, drowning their uncertainty or anger
in food and song. But a critic intent on eliciting an earnest reading of
an apparently earnest and possibly unsophisticated ethnic author will
understandably overlook those contradictions.

Furthermore, because I come from an exotic and attractive back-ground, I fell immediately into the uncomfortable position of won-dering whether the literary community would value my work only to the extent that I continued to represent that background. The interest in enlarging the literary canon to include multicultural voices not only made it possible for a book like *Sleeping Preacher* to be published, but it also made me wonder whether that interest was the only reason for its success. My personal anxiety was simply assumed by poet David Wojahn in an essay in which he explored the dire state of first book publication in America. Pointing out that the few first books of poetry that go into second or third printings often do so for reasons that have little to do with their literary merit, he wrote, "Julia Kasdorf's *Sleeping Preacher* found a sales niche among the Mennonite commu-nities where its poems are set, no doubt because the book's ambiva-lent stance toward the speaker's heritage created something of a scan-dal. Nothing like the *Peyton Place* effect to move a little poetry, and the poems must have seemed especially titillating within a community where having cable is regarded as a sin."[9] And nothing like a little gra-tuitous generalization to spice up one's writing.

Although I'm sure my book has sold more copies outside the Men-nonite community than within it, I did imagine that subsequent col-lections, if they were to be equally successful, needed to spring from that background. But a life is shaped by many things, and if *Sleeping Preacher* was written as an attempt to examine and understand the stories that shaped my ethnic identity, then *Eve's Striptease* was an at-tempt to do the same with the stories that shaped my sexual and gen-dered identity. Ironically, the second book has been seen by some as less daring; a New York University creative writing teacher told me in the late 1980s, "Anyone can write about sex, but who wants to talk about religion? That is the real taboo." A glance at current works of fic-tion and nonfiction suggests that readers may now be more ready to approach that taboo topic.

Yet a brief review of *Eve's Striptease* that appeared in a major New York–based reviewing service is so caustic along these lines as to be illuminating. The unnamed writer finds the few traces of "Mennonite simplicity" in the poems "charming in their way" but attributes the failure of the majority of the book to linguistic and imaginative deficiencies that are the consequence of Protestant repression. Identifying me in the first sentence as "the Messiah College teacher," the reviewer laments the "poor sexual education" evident in poems about the body and complains that, even when Brooklyn's "sounds and colors challenge the drabness of her Protestant background," they cannot rescue such dull poems. In conclusion, the reviewer writes, "Kasdorf's modesty and naivete prevail and prevent real passion."[10] To be a WASP is to be emotionally shut down and a bad artist, but to be Mennonite is to be exotic and even vaguely erotic, as Wojahn's *Peyton Place* quip illustrates. Think of Kelly McGillis as the young Amish widow who bares her breasts for the Philadelphia detective—and the camera—in the film aptly titled *Witness*. Or consider my friend Christie, an NYU graduate student of cinema studies, who took one look at the cover of my first book and announced, "She's masturbating under that quilt!" The ethnic woman—whether black or gold or brown or wrapped in an Amish quilt—becomes erotic in the popular imagination.

Picture/Window

In David's painting, the religious and ethnic community is represented by a man in traditional dress and a horse and buggy, enclosed within a tight frame located above the woman's body. The man sees a conversation between the secular literary scene, represented by the book, and a reclining Mennonite daughter, who has suddenly become an author through the publication of the book that bears her name.

For the most part, my work has been celebrated by the Mennonite community. People plan and attend readings in churches and denominational colleges and public spaces, and afterward some have sent encouraging and touching confessional letters of gratitude. They tell me stories and greet me with warmth and an attitude of collusion as they wait for me to sign their books. It seems as if they feel they know me or are known by me, and they seem filled with gratitude. At these times, I have thought of novelist Don Belton and a story he told me from his growing up in the 1960s in Philadelphia. Some afternoons, he said, a kid would run down the block, shouting with great excitement to anyone on the stoop or hanging out of the windows, "Colored people on television! Colored people on television!" And then everyone would go inside and turn on the set, just to see them. Maybe some Mennonite readers are that eager to read any representation of themselves in literature.

For me, the enthusiastic attention has complicated and conflicted meanings. On the one hand, I know that I am viewed as a point of pride, someone who managed to succeed in the wider world as an articulate representative of the group. On the other hand, I may appear to be an unreliable or even dangerous representative, so my work must be claimed and domesticated. Because there have been so few representations of Mennonites in mainstream literature, new publications naturally create some anxiety about issues of textual accuracy as well as author intent and authenticity—including her membership status in the community.

The most artful and subtle expression of this anxiety is an introduction John Ruth wrote for a reading I gave in his home community in eastern Pennsylvania in 1994. I was living in New York City at the time, apparently outside the Mennonite sphere. But for an audience located in North America's oldest rural Mennonite settlement, John managed to situate me in relation to the American Mennonite story and to place my work in line with previous Mennonite literature, even while asserting the distinctive contribution that my writing may now make. "Although two decades before there was a *Martyrs Mirror* there were Dutch Mennonites in Manhattan, they left no records, no statement of their identity; their presence was recorded by others," he began. Next, he visited the docks at Philadelphia where three boatloads of Swiss Anabaptist ancestors arrived without any written texts and spoke a dialect so thick that even the German-speaking Mennonites could not understand them, so "they disappeared into the woods without so much as registering their names." (One of their ministers did commission the translation and printing of *Martyrs Mirror* and encourage some writings on pedagogy, but colonial American Mennonite leaders confessed to their Dutch brothers that they were too busy even to keep records in the New World.) Then, in his introduction, John turned to the Pennsylvania Dutch–inflected English common to Amish-Mennonite communities, which has occasionally been extracted from the Amish newspaper the *Budget* and used as comical filler in the *New Yorker*:

> What we have in Julia Spicher Kasdorf is a heart that has brought the language of the *Budget* from the bottom to the top of the page, as she muses in lovely language on the Amish-Mennonite *Freundschaft* it's almost impossible to articulate in any language than poetic. . . .
>
> Julia's lovingly quizzical poems recall for me a blasé New York voice on the telephone, from CBS. Charles Kuralt was about to narrate on "Sixty Minutes" some footage Burton Buller and I had shot of Amish life. Apparently he or some other urban expert wanted to know, "Are you sure it isn't pronounced Aymish?"
>
> Julia lives affectionately among people who neither understand nor are understood by her own people. . . . Living in Babylon, Julia has continued to nurture an idiom whose simplicity belies its depth.[11]

As with nearly all of John's utterances—oral or written—his introduction contains witty anecdotes and rich details from community history, blending a boastful pride of heritage with regret for its slight literary tradition. It was flattering to receive this quality of attention from an articulate patriarch, and I recall being moved as I listened that afternoon. The message seemed a warm and generous welcome home, as persuasive as one of John Ruth's Sunday sermons, and expressive of a desire to forge continuity between tradition and literary innovation, that is, between community and individual. Afterward, he gave me a copy of the speech, and only later did I see how complicated its meanings are. Is this text a speedy redemption for a writer who believed that she needed to leave her community in order to find enough quiet to think her own thoughts, who felt that she had committed transgres-

MENNONITES

We keep our quilts in closets and do not dance.
We hoe thistles along fence rows for fear
we may not be perfect as our Heavenly Father.
We clean up his disasters. No one has to
call; we just show up in the wake of tornadoes
with hammers, after floods with buckets.
Like Jesus, the servant, we wash each other's feet
twice a year and eat the Lord's Supper,
afraid of sins hidden so deep in our organs
they could damn us unawares,
swallowing this bread, his body, this juice.
Growing up, we love the engravings in *Martyrs Mirror:*
Men drowned like cats in burlap sacks,
the Catholic inquisitors,
the woman who handed a pear to her son,
her tongue screwed to the roof of her mouth
to keep her from singing hymns while she burned.
We love Catherine the Great and the rich tracts
she gave us in the Ukraine, bright green winter wheat,

sion by writing at all? For whom—the audience or myself—was this survey of local Mennonite literary history and peaceful restoration of a prodigal author made?

Although John casually mentions that he too makes representations of Anabaptist people—films that violate Amish photography taboos—I am cast in relation to a world beyond the community, due not only to the location of my poems in the *New Yorker,* but also to the location of my body in New York City, among "urban experts" who misunderstand our *Freundschaft* (kin) and mispronounce its words. I am figured as a hero who can elevate the status of our plain, homely language. Although he sees me "living in Babylon," John enfolds me in the community's quilt, which becomes a protective sheath, as if my

the Cossacks who torched it, and Stalin,
who starved our cousins while wheat rotted
in granaries. We must love our enemies.
We must forgive as our sins are forgiven,
our great-uncle tells us, showing the chain
and ball in a cage whittled from one block of wood
while he was in prison for refusing to shoulder
a gun. He shows the clipping from 1916:
Mennonites are German milksops, too yellow to fight.
We love those Nazi soldiers who, like Moses,
led the last cattle cars rocking out of Ukraine,
crammed with our parents—children then—
learning the names of Kansas, Saskatchewan, Paraguay.
This is why we cannot leave the beliefs
or what else would we be? why we eat
'til we're drunk on shoofly and moon pies and borscht.
We do not drink; we sing. Unaccompanied on Sundays,
those hymns in four parts, our voices lift with such force
that we lift, as chaff lifts toward God.

work could remain untainted by Babylonian experience. John thus speaks as the man in the window/picture above the bed, charging me with a communal vocation and swiftly grafting my book onto the slim stalk of Mennonite literature. Although it is nice to feel welcome and have one's work respected, there is also something troubling about being claimed this directly and bound to tradition this simply. Are the poems that I recall writing with bitter tears, nostalgia often a mask for anger hidden so deep as to be wrenching and unrecognizable, really "lovingly quizzical"?

For instance, "Mennonites" was written all at once in a rushed response to feelings of alienation in my graduate poetry workshop. In retrospect, I see that this poem conflates all Mennonite people—of

Swiss and Dutch origins, of the Russian and American migrations, plain and acculturated—into one mass "we." Ethnic foods and historical details drawn from my own background and that of my husband blend together as distinct ethnic identities collapse, the way an outsider might fail to differentiate between distinct groups within a broader religious tradition—viewing all Ashkenazi and Sephardic people as Jewish, for instance. The immediate energy of "Mennonites" comes from a frustrated desire to sort out identity questions about my ethnic and religious community of memory, but within the presence of secular readers who were the poem's first audience.

What does the Mennonite community gain by reading such poems as "lovingly quizzical" or failing to see that they were written in tense conversation with a wider world? Perhaps one answer to this question can be gathered from community responses to the appearance of "Mennonites" in *Many Worlds of Literature*. Roger Kurtz, son of Mennonite missionaries and university professor of postcolonial and multicultural literature, ironically posted the discussion notes from the instructor's manual of *Many Worlds of Literature* with little comment of his own on Mennolink, the electronic mail listserv that sustains informal and obsessive banter about things Mennonite. The textbook's statements, cited here in part, direct readers to notice "evident" expressions of culture in the poem. A student following these guidelines would glean from the poem only the usual stereotype of Mennonite people as rural, clannish, religiously devout, hardworking, and socially separatist:

1. Mennonites prefer a rural setting to an urban one . . . consistent with their isolationist mentality since a rural area is often cut off from the rest of the world. In these types of areas, they can live as they please.
2. The Mennonite way of life is very community-oriented. Selfishness is frowned upon. This is evident from the use of the term "we" instead of the more common "I" by the speaker.
3. It is evident that the Mennonites hold themselves to very high standards, standards that outsiders may consider overly severe . . . The Mennonites seem to actually practice what they preach.

4. . . . The metaphor of the harvest develops the idea of single-minded devotion to God since both activities require dedication, sacrifice, and hard work.[12]

J. Lorne Peachey, editor of the Mennonite news magazine *Gospel Herald,* saw Roger Kurtz's Mennolink posting and used it—along with *Taste of Home,* a cooking publication that listed the denominational affiliation of only its Mennonite contributor—as the occasion for an editorial expressive of double consciousness and titled with a line of antique English from Robert Burns, "To see ourselvs as ithers see us!" Peachey challenged his readers to match the high ideals expressed in the popular cultural stereotypes.[13] I was baffled that this editor—my mother's second cousin, who taught me how to pull taffy when I was a child and listened sympathetically to my adolescent frustrations—would rely on a textbook writer to interpret my poem, although he had plenty of emotional and experiential information to form his own reading. Perhaps his was only a response to a literary expert, or an example of another writer exercising selective interpretive strategies for his own purposes.

In a 1997 essay describing the emergence of Mennonite poetry in the early 1990s, Jeff Gundy used this episode to illustrate the ways that Mennonite church leaders invoke—and perhaps willfully misread—the community's few publishing poets:

> Lorne Peachey's *Gospel Herald* editorial pays much closer attention to the teacher's guide for the anthology and what it reveals about the way "others" see "us" than to Julia Kasdorf's poem itself. He notes with considerable satisfaction the statements in the "discussion notes" that Mennonites have "a single-minded devotion to God" and "seem to actually practice what they preach." Both Peachey and the anthologist seem oblivious to the understated but radical irony of the poem. . . . In its quiet way the poem raises fundamental questions about who and what Mennonites are; it challenges the very complacency that Peachey attempts, perhaps unwittingly, to restore.[14]

A NEW MENNONITE REPLIES TO JULIA KASDORF
David Wright

> This is why we cannot leave the beliefs
> or what else would we be?
> —Julia Kasdorf, from "Mennonites"

As best I can tell, most of our quilts here were inherited,
or bought at relief sales, spread on guest beds
and splayed on shiny oak racks. Not much borscht,
few shoofly pies at potlucks—instead it's
hummus, free-range chicken, carob brownies.
No bacon-laced bean casserole. Someone
steamed soybeans last Sunday, right in the pods.

Maundy Thursday we wash each other's hands.
It is optional, so I stay seated,
beside a Lutheran woman, Harvard
theologian, and we wish together
for liturgy because we cannot play
the name game. Neither can my agnostic
Quaker friend. We drink coffee on Mondays
to talk politics instead. Between fields,
one farmer, ex-Amish and an Otto
brother, teaches medieval Catholic
thinkers whose names I can never recall.

So many new and remade and restless
and not-quite Mennonites, driving Volvos
and minivans. We park ourselves in pews
next to women and men who know better
what real Mennonites really are, at least
have usually been, who tolerate us
when we do not know or want to the so

many stories we should. Some seem amused,
some even grieved, others simply angry
that our martyr stories come in children's
sermons where Dirk rescues and is killed right
next to Rosa Parks and Ruby Bridges,
where Luther himself nails necessary
correctives on Wittenberg's door.

We sing,
though, a solid four parts; the hymns here have
a sturdy bottom (though I need the book
on 606). And we make our way through
less solid but sweet guitar-sent songs
your great-uncles would never recognize.
Our preacher never swoons. He's biblical,
careful, and knows the university
crowd listens each week. Once, he prayed, "May God
bless your mind's wanderings." Which go now to
China Buffet, where two tables away
a woman wears heavy head covering
and pale green dress as she eats with her son.
I say to Becky, "Should we tell her?" "What?"
"That we're Mennonites too?" Becky smiles, licks
sugar from her fingers, the residue
of deep fried dough passing here for ethnic
dessert—"Maybe we could tell her we're new
at it?" God bless our wandering, indeed.[15]

As evidence for his reading, Gundy focuses on the end of the poem, where ethnic food and four-part singing—emblems of Mennonite identity—threaten to dissolve in the final line, " . . . we lift, as chaff lifts toward God." I am told that this line puzzled several readers at a Mennonite college faculty retreat so much that they finally concluded that the author did not know the meaning of the word *chaff*.

In their minds, it was more likely that I would misuse a word than metaphorically compare our community to chaff which, in biblical parables, is analogous to the sinful or worthless and, separated from the useful grain, blows away or is cast into the fire.

A final response to "Mennonites" comes from Illinois poet and college professor, David Wright, a Mennonite by choice rather than birth. His poem, which was published by Peachey in the same denominational magazine that printed the editorial, ably resists the impulse to confuse Mennonite identity with emblems of ethnicity, offering an alternative, authentic image of the "new Mennonite"—as opposed to Gundy's parodic "new Mennonite poem."

I see in this poem an effective critique of the ethnocentric certainty of those "who know better/what real Mennonites really are." The new Mennonite is not *Freundschaft* and is therefore left out of "the name game," a conversational tick that repeatedly establishes common ground by naming common acquaintances, especially blood relatives. Unburdened by the stories and freight of inheritance, the new vision is nonetheless grounded in the material world and more broadly inclusive: whether the quilts are purchased or inherited, they are spread on a bed for guests; European Anabaptist martyrs are no more sacred than African-American civil rights hero Rosa Parks; the thoughtful pastor does not preach from a trance but blesses the wandering minds in his congregation; and plain-dressed and converted Mennonites eat together in a Chinese restaurant. This utopian vision of decentered authority is deeply democratic, hospitable, and cosmopolitan, curiously akin to the Anabaptist view of a community of believers bound to one another by personal choice and common commitment.

Woman

In David's painting, there is a meaningful confusion about who the sleeping preacher is: the female lying in bed or the patriarch in the window. The actual sleeping preachers were trance speakers active more than a hundred years ago in the United States and Scandinavia. They were always nonordained, unsanctioned voices—sometimes they were even women. In the years after the American Civil War, Anabaptist groups and other Christian denominations experienced splintering stresses about matters of religious belief and practice. During this tumultuous period, in farm communities from Iowa to Virginia, Amish and Mennonite people gathered to listen to the mysterious trance sermons. There is record of audiences of more than a thousand in attendance at these meetings. The preachers were said to possess special knowledge during the trance state that they did not have when they were awake, and afterward they had no memory of the sermon they had preached. No one knew whether they were fakes or authentic messengers from God, but just to be safe, the community did not silence them. Therefore, the sleeping preacher seemed an apt metaphor for a poet who comes from my background.[16]

This moves me to reflect on the reclining woman, whom I take to represent myself in the role of author. Her eyes are closed, suggesting that she doesn't quite see what she is doing as she writes from imagination, memory, or dreams. "What is essential is invisible to the eye," says the Little Prince in Antoine de Saint-Exupéry's wise storybook.[17] "We are all blind," Yehuda Amichai told our poetry workshop at NYU, "but the poetry you write is like a seeing eye dog that leads you around in the world." I have often thought of writing as a partly unconscious act, done mostly in the dark; the poetry seems always to be smarter than I am, and most days I feel that I am not very bright. After readings, I am frequently surprised and grateful when comments from an audience member suddenly help me to understand the meanings a poem carries. Revising, I have learned to trust an intuitive sense of completion even when I can't quite explain to myself why a poem feels finished. Because the process of writing poetry is organic and its logic unfolds associatively, it rarely conforms to the linear, discursive forms of theology or history; therefore, it cannot engage directly with the traditional discourses of authority in my community. And yet my poems sometimes call that authority into question.

That authority is personified as a plain-dressed man in David's painting. Although his eyes are lowered, he seems to be watching me in a pose that could be protective, possessive, or even predatory. Of course, as long as my eyes are closed, I cannot tell the difference. So I must eventually open my eyes, wake from trance or dissociation to face those figures. I must learn how to converse in a world that, for the sake of its survival, must sometimes check the utterances of its members. Growing up in a congregation affiliated with the Mennonite Publishing House, I did not miss the point that editors of adult literature were also ordained men. The male body that Eve strides out of, "sloughing off ribs," in the title poem of my second book isn't an abstraction, a friend has wisely observed; it is the church figured as a Mennonite Adam.

But the striptease is incomplete. I still occasionally feel uncertain about the ways that writing exposes my thoughts—and often my body—to the eyes of others. Modesty is construed as a virtue, even in art. I think of W. H. Auden's introduction to Adrienne Rich's first book, which expressed this value in terms of her person as well as her work: "Miss Rich, who is, I understand, twenty-one years old, displays a modesty not so common at that age, which disclaims any extraordinary vision." Later in the introduction he concluded that "the poems a reader will encounter in this book are neatly and modestly dressed, speak quietly but do not mumble, respect their elders but are not cowed by them, and do not tell fibs: that, for a first volume, is a good deal."[18] In 1951, one might expect the work of a female poet to be compared to a body; one might expect a female to be praised for writing poems that respect authority. But why am I still haunted by this hideous praise?

Perhaps there is some connection between a sense of modesty in dress, including my choice to wear the prayer veil as a young woman, and the feelings of shame and depression that I used to get after giving public readings, especially those that seemed to have been successful. Those times, I wanted to hide from the audience, to slip out a back door during their applause rather than sign books and receive compliments. With Virginia Woolf in *A Room of One's Own,* I could claim that "publicity in women is detestable. Anonymity runs in their blood. The desire to be veiled still possesses them."[19] This desire is not of our own making; we have learned it from cultures that seek to veil us. I think of the Mennonite friend who invited me to give a reading after the publication of my second book but then had trouble finding an auditorium in her community because no one could risk offending conservative donors who supported the local Mennonite cultural institutions. One idea was to hold the reading in a barn—a nice, remodeled barn—but the resemblance to another time when only a stable was available struck me as too strange, so I suggested that the sponsors advertise the reading without mentioning *Eve's Striptease* by name. Recently, after having written a book endorsement, I learned that the Mennonite publisher of that book would not print the words *Eve's Striptease* to identify me on the jacket, out of fear or respect for conservative readers. Finally, weary of such selective appropriations of my life and writing, I asked that they use my words, name, and book title—or nothing at all. They chose nothing, which is surely a publisher's prerogative.

As the sleeping girl in the painting wakes up, she gains more control over her own representation—like the stripper in Sylvia Plath's "Lady Lazarus," who self-consciously camps her performance for a curious "peanut-crunching crowd." If earlier books sought to understand and resist the scripts of ethnicity and gender, these essays attempt to understand and revise the female ethnic author's role. Thus, I have tried to climb out of the corner that pinched me between the traditional community and my literary ambition. I no longer see the window in opposition to the book on the chair. I understand that I first entered the literary world because I had written a book about my traditional background, and people who share that background are an important and sustaining audience. But I move through the world as an individual, not merely as a member of a group.

My experience with authority in the religious community nonetheless helps me to negotiate between the forms of power that I encounter in my dealings with literary critics and editors; the sense of mutual aid I learned within the Mennonite community is frequently enacted in my relationships with members of the literary community.

I have some access to both communities, and they occasionally blur and overlap through sustaining friendships with artists of Mennonite and other traditional backgrounds. Writing essays has helped me to climb outside the frame of this painting, to try to make meaning of the sight. Out here with you, dear reader, I find that I worry less about how I can be myself and inhabit these two communities, because this vantage point allows me to see and consider many things beyond this picture.

CAMP HILL, 1999

We begged you, Lord, to divide right from wrong
and instead you divided the waters above the firmament
from those beneath it.

YEHUDA AMICHAI, "The Course of a Life"

Bodies and Boundaries

6

From the time of Paul and the early church, Christians have imagined their religious communities to be human bodies metaphorically figured as the Body of Christ or the Bride of Christ. I wonder whether this metaphor has shaped and limited the ways that groups relate to others, even as it could suggest new possibilities for relationship. Among my earliest memories of such a metaphoric body is a small group of Mennonite graduate students and young professionals who gathered for fellowship in a University of Pittsburgh classroom. There were chalkboards and desks with molded plastic seats, and casseroles were lined up on a window sill. Some time later, the group began meeting in the Rodef Shalom synagogue near Shady Side. Only once or twice did I catch a glimpse of the glorious, darkened sanctuary upstairs because the thick wooden doors were almost always sealed on Sunday mornings when Mennonites gathered in the basement. After those services, my family often visited Carnegie Institute, where dinosaur bones and cases of

Epigraph: Chana Bloch and Stephen Mitchell, ed. and trans., *The Selected Poetry of Yehuda Amichai* (New York: HarperCollins, 1986), 156.

exotic butterflies inscribed on my imagination another kind of scripture. Maybe this is why I have followed a spiritual path that leads out of doors, through urban universities, and into other people's houses of worship. Maybe this is why I believe that the dominion of God is nearly boundless, and communion should be more like a potluck than an exclusive dinner party.

But also among my first memories of a gathered body of believers is Locust Grove, a Conservative Conference congregation in Mifflin County, Pennsylvania. The old meetinghouse, which no longer exists, was a white frame structure with plain blond benches and an amen corner. Men and women sat on separate sides of the center aisle, and the only ornament was a sober, white-faced clock above the pulpit, like the clock that hung above a row of perfect cursive letters that framed the blackboard at my grammar school. The Sunday I'm thinking of must have been long before I attended school, though. For that communion service, people silently knelt on the floor to pray, heads in hands, heavy bosoms pressing against forearms on the bench seat. It was a little frightening to see grown women in this condition. Were they crying? Peering under the bench, I was shocked to discover things I was sure I'd never seen before. At first, I was so disoriented that I couldn't figure out what I was looking at, but then it suddenly hit me: the bottoms of hundreds of Mennonite women's sensible shoes! Wide and dark and scuffed—so strange, they made me think of cows' and horses' hooves.

I was confused and troubled by the solemn atmosphere of that meetinghouse, where, as baskets of bread cubes and trays of tiny tumblers of grape juice silently passed hand to hand down the pew, communion reminded people of suffering—not just the passion of the crucifixion, but the pain of the sacrifices each of them made every day. Such a community of faith is like a loaf of bread, composed of many grains of wheat that must be ground together; it is like wine pressed from many individual grapes. Just as each grain of wheat must be pulverized and each grape must likewise be crushed, so must it be with the members of the Body of Christ, according to an important

The white frame meeting house of the Locust Grove Mennonite Church, Mifflin County, Pennsylvania, was razed in 1973. The silo on the lower right belongs to the farm where my mother grew up and where I lived the first few months of my life.

Anabaptist metaphor. It is impossible for whole kernels to be a true part of the bread and for whole grapes to mingle their juices in the wine.[1] The ache of that human marmalade, a metaphor as ancient as the early Church, has stayed with me as a reminder of the cost of belonging to the Body of Christ.

In those days, the faithful wore signs of belonging on their bodies every day. If they were men, that belonging may have showed in the cut of their coats. For women, it was sewn in the length of their skirts and sleeves, in the cape, a flap of fabric that concealed their breasts; and it rested on their heads, covering their buns with white net. If someone had moved away and cut her hair, as my mother had, she might ask the hairdresser to fashion a chignon out of the clippings. She'd store that tight, round knot in the cedar chest and, through some ingenious womanly art, manage to pin it back on her head whenever she returned to Locust Grove. To belong to the Body of Christ was so important that she'd gladly alter her own body. This was not physical torture or martyrdom exactly; it was just how one member chose to conform so that she could show others, and know herself, that she belonged to a group that was not conformed to the ways of the world.

Sitting on the bench among grandmas and aunts and great-aunts and cousins, both distant and close, I knew that belonging to the Body had more than metaphoric or spiritual meanings. I belonged with the people in that congregation because I was literally related to them: we experienced the Body of Christ as an extension of our own ancestry and physiology. Although other Christians may have seen a figure of speech in 1 Corinthians 12:27 ("Now ye are the body of Christ, and members in particular"), Mennonites in deeply rooted rural communities could claim that the church was one body in actuality. Members shared not only history, religious beliefs, and practices with other people in the community, but also they shared genetic material. This sense of connection reaches powerfully across time as contemporary Mennonites can claim a spiritual and physical heritage in sixteenth-century Anabaptism. "The blood of martyrs flows in our veins," H. S. Bender would tell his Goshen College students who were descended from Swiss Mennonite immigrants.[2] To be enmeshed with a blood community like this can feel pleasurable, comfortable, and secure. To pull away from such a community is to risk losing a part of one's self. Because the community's members draw their individual identities from a sense of relationship with the community, to withdraw or be expelled from such a group can feel like a dismemberment or amputation, like a suicide or homicide.

In the fall of 1997, after lengthy deliberations and threats that several congregations might leave the denomination in protest, delegates of the Franconia Conference of the Mennonite Church chose to vote by mail-in ballot whether to expel the Germantown Mennonite Church because of that congregation's willingness to accept into its membership openly gay and lesbian people. As we waited for the decision, I boldly predicted that, because of a pride of history and blood, the conference would never excommunicate the oldest Mennonite church in North America. Founded in 1683, this congregation supported the first formal protest against slavery in the New World, and now the small church in Philadelphia is metaphorically and actually populated by children of larger, traditional Mennonite churches in rural areas north of the city. I insisted that blood runs thicker than the waters of Mennonite baptism or the heterosexist sentiments of conservative Christianity. I believed that Mennonites would never cast their own children out of fellowship. Perhaps they wouldn't have if the vote had been taken in the customary fashion, at a public gathering of all the delegates rather than by secret ballot—or, as later rumors reported, if conservative congregations with few historic Mennonite families had not been involved. When I checked my email on the morning of October 15, a press release prepared by members of the Germantown congregation shocked me to tears. That the congregational site of a seventeenth-century human rights protest could not now speak to one of the most pressing human rights issues of the moment struck me as a particularly cruel irony, which was later implied in a National Public Radio story about the case. But my sense of it all was more visceral than that.

When Linda Parkyn, the chair of my department at Messiah College, wandered into my office, I had to explain why I was weeping at my computer. Folding me into a motherly embrace, she soothed, "It's OK. You're an Episcopalian now." But the ache I felt that day and afterward, as if part of my own self had been torn off, suggested that my body would always be Mennonite, and that what had happened to that congregation had also happened to me.

Some Implications of the Body Metaphor

As my earliest and deeply dissonant memories of two Pennsylvania Mennonite worship services reveal, the traditional community of blood and faith relations had already begun to disintegrate or diversify by the late 1960s. Many American Mennonites now consider the material markers that identified the conservative community—distinctive language, dress, and lifestyle—to be distant or irrelevant memories, yet I know that some kind of birthright Mennonite identity still persists. A distinct cultural sense is still signaled by feelings of connection; unspoken expressions of taste, memory, and value; and shared understandings about where the community begins and ends. That invisible boundary, with few exceptions, follows genetic lines, what some Mennonites still call *Freundschaft*. What began as a free movement of the Spirit has become a denomination bound by memory and blood, although how deep that blood still flows remains to be seen. In a global demographic view of the denomination, the most representative Mennonite at the beginning of the twenty-first century is an African woman. Nonetheless, in North American communities with European roots, physical experience and the ancient and powerful body metaphor shape perceptions of the religious community. Paradoxically, this metaphor may thwart the community's deepest desire, which is to love others.

My consideration of the body metaphor is inspired by the work of the linguistic philosophers George Lakoff and Mark Johnson, who assert that the physical experience of our own bodies shapes our metaphoric ways of thinking and that a culture's most important values will be aligned with the metaphorical structures of its fundamental concepts. Lakoff and Johnson have demonstrated numerous ways in which particular metaphors control perception by accenting some aspects of a concept and masking others. For instance, because we metaphorically figure argument as war, we approach discussions with a certain set of unconscious assumptions; and these assumptions structure our experience and shape our behavior in those situations. If we were able to employ the metaphor of dance, on the other hand, we would probably approach such conversations quite differently.[3]

As human beings who experience our physical bodies as distinct entities possessing insides and outsides, it naturally follows that we would experience a group, metaphorically figured as a body, as a being that is distinct and manifest through its physical boundaries. The experience of physical health—a body whose boundaries have not been penetrated by injury or infection—shapes this image of community purity, wellness, and wholeness. Therefore, it may even be that the primary property of such a metaphoric body is its boundaries, and the only imaginable ways of being in relation to such a body are either inside or outside its bounds. Inside is good, pure, true; outside is bad. I think of lines from the smug Sunday school song: "One door and only one, and yet its sides are two. / I'm on the inside. On which side are you?"

Of course, this inside/outside mentality is common to many groups. Allegiance to protecting boundaries and bounded identities seems to be everywhere and to be at the center of much of the violence on our planet. Whether they are engaged in gang skirmishes or genocidal wars, individuals strive to preserve a sense of self by defending the boundaries that define group identity. Though Mennonites are not willing to take up arms and thereby betray one of the group's most essential boundary markers, like other groups, they are capable of violating the interests of others in order to protect a sense of self, especially a collective self. Through gestures of dogma and dismissal, by refusing to listen to others, by stubbornly retracing the boundaries that define community identity, individuals enact the human behaviors that are antithetical to the ethic Mennonites claim to value most—nonresistant love.

Yet also within the body metaphor lies the hope of transcending the limits of the bounded body. Whereas bodies do have insides and outsides, experience suggests that they have many other qualities as well. Perhaps the most profound aspect of human experience is that we live in relationship. As infants, we first learn to recognize our mothers and fathers. We receive our names from others; others teach us language and culture; our survival and quality of life always depend on how well we develop and negotiate relationships. I wonder what would happen if communities were regarded, not primarily as bounded entities, but as bodies capable and always in need of relationship—as individuals are? What could be learned if we applied to communities some understandings about individual identity and the dynamics of relationship between self and other?

A question that immediately arises for me is whether Mennonites would regard the group as the self or the other. It seems that Anabaptists are probably most comfortable thinking of their community as the other, following in the path of the sixteenth-century martyrs, a prophetic counterculture set against the wider, fallen world. Yet the bounded body must always be the powerful *One* for its constituting members who strive to retain their sense of belonging. And, as Simone de Beauvoir points out, "No group ever sets itself up as the One without at once setting up the Other over against itself."[4] Such a relationship is characterized by opposition. Boundaries function as borders that serve to preserve and define distinction—whether the other be a deviant insider or a friendly stranger. Without others pressing against its boundaries, the way flying buttresses keep cathedral walls from crumbling, the community would have no sense of its own shape. The body needs others to know itself, and it continues to know itself through relationship.

Mikhail Bakhtin

Current thinking that regards the human body as the site where individual identity is socially constructed has led me to speculate about an analogous principle concerning the way group identity is made and preserved. Particularly helpful has been the early writing of Mikhail Bakhtin, a literary theorist and philosopher from the Eastern Orthodox tradition, who is best known for his later work on the novel and discourse.[5] While still in his twenties, during the creative postrevolutionary years before the rise of Stalin, he wrote the essays and fragments collected in *Art and Answerability* and gave public lectures on philosophy and Christianity. In one debate, he charged that socialism "shows no concern for the dead" and that in time, "people won't forgive that."[6] The reason given for his 1929 arrest was membership in *Voskresenie* (Resurrection), an organization that sought to integrate Christian beliefs and Marxist thought. On the eve of the purges of the 1930s, Bakhtin's public appearances and writings (sometimes published under the names of friends) eventually resulted in his exile to a provincial teaching post, which he held in relative obscurity until his retirement in the early 1960s.[7]

In "Author and Hero in Aesthetic Activity," Bakhtin begins with an experience common to most human beings: vision. Caryl Emerson suggests that Bakhtin's theoretical grounding in the physical act of seeing reflects the Russian Orthodox tradition wherein the spirit is nurtured as much by the eye as by the book. Whereas for Christians in the West, biblical meanings are bound to the text, in the East an image may hold as much meaning as the Word. In fact, images and icons are so important in worship and religious practice that they may precede intellectual understandings gained through reading Scripture or spoken sermons. A tradition of religious art and aesthetic consciousness has long flourished in the Orthodox world because the incarnation is precedent and model for artistic creation. The artistic act imitates the incarnation as word (idea) becomes flesh (material), and flesh (material experience) becomes image or text. Further extending this principle, the incarnation suggests an ethics grounded in creation and aesthetics. This ethics follows a Creator God who, in the words of the Israeli poet Amichai, first divided "the waters above the firmament from those beneath it," instead of sorting right from wrong.[8]

Bakhtin first notes that we are never able to observe the entire surface of our own bodies. Only another person can see my body all at once in relation to its environment. The other's privileged perspective he calls "an excess of knowing." Only an other, looking with concentrated attention, can "consummate" me—make me whole—know me as I cannot know myself. For Bakhtin, "consummation" in interpersonal relations is an aesthetic activity that first involves respect and knowledge of the exterior contours that constitute a person's physical form. But consummation also includes some knowledge of the contours that define an other's inner being, the other's soul or inner form. Such profound seeing and listening can only happen from a specific point of view in the real world—and it will likely transform the other. In one of my favorite passages in the essay, Bakhtin describes this action:

> After all, it is only the other who can be embraced, clasped all around, it is only the other's boundaries that can all be touched and felt lovingly. The other's fragile finiteness, consummatedness, his here-and-now being—all

are inwardly grasped by me and shaped, as it were, by my embrace; in this act, the other's outward existence begins to live in a new manner, acquires some sort of new meaning, is born on a new plane of being. Only the other's lips can be touched with our own, only on the other can we lay our hands, rise actively above the other and "overshadow" all of him totally, "overshadow" him in every constituent feature of his existence, "overshadow" his body and within his body—his soul.[9]

The language of this passage trembles in that highly charged territory where intellectual and physical intercourse meet in spiritual consummation. The translator of the text, Vadim Liapunov, notes that in Russian, *overshadow* means "the power to shelter, protect, and bless," as in Luke 1:35: "The Holy Ghost shall come upon thee, and the power of the Highest shall overshadow thee." In that scene, the angel explains to Mary that God's "overshadowing" will cause her to become pregnant. The quality of the relationship between self and another beyond the self is an overshadowing, interpenetrating love so powerful it results in change. Bakhtin notes that God—the ultimate Other—is the most powerful, most perfect practitioner of this kind of attention.

Here it seems important to note that, in an essay that is profoundly idealistic, Bakhtin regards lust as the violation of an other's boundaries. Although it may involve moments of loving and aesthetic admiration for the other, this gaze "disintegrates" the other's outer body, transforming it into that which is only a constituent of the viewer's inner body. In such a situation, another being's value is only recognized in connection with the possibilities of my own desire, pleasure, and gratification. Undesired or unbidden, this gaze captures and attempts to possess. Yet as a male intellectual writing in an optimistic era, Bakhtin seems to assume that the other's gaze usually will be ethical and benevolent, or that the self will be strong enough to discern and resist whatever destructive definitions will be projected upon it.[10] Although he does not consider the source of such strength and discernment, elsewhere Bakhtin refers to God as the ultimate Other. If God's love consummates the self as worthy, it will then be strengthened to resist the biased limits that will be projected upon it. For instance, a sense of self-worth and empowerment drawn from knowing themselves to be children of God enabled some members of the African-American community to resist racism and apartheid during the Civil Rights movement. Additionally, the consummating love and comfort of others help one to resist and wisely discern such diminishing definitions. Unlike lust, the ethical-aesthetic impulse seeks always to restore meaning and wholeness for the other.

So the command "love your neighbor as yourself" is an impossibility. We can never love or "consummate" ourselves; only another can do this. As the infant learns her name from others, so we continuously depend on others to give us information about ourselves, to construct our identities, and to provide meaning for our lives. From inside our own bodies and inside the limits of our existence, we experience only a vague unknowing; we can only imagine possibilities for ourselves. Through loving relationships, however, others provide us with information. And as we come to accumulate many images of who we are, we continuously construct and revise a sense of self. Whatever identity we have at a given time is the result of our inner consciousness in conversation with the images others have provided from their outward experience of us. The gift others give to us is the recognition and construction of an individual self. And our own sense of identity is based on the ability to keep a self intact.

This idea is strikingly illustrated by an event described in *Going by the Moon and the Stars,* Pamela Klassen's ethnographic study of the life stories of two Mennonite women who escaped Soviet Russia at the end of World War II. Katja Enns (pseudonym), barely twenty years old, is pregnant with the child of a German soldier. Starving and alone, she is strafed by an American fighter in Germany. These are her words:

> They always come in three, squadrons of three.
> And all of a sudden one turned off, saw me walking on the road and
> started to shoot at me.
> There was a big tree—

and again, when I think of it, it must be God's way to guide me,

because I ran to that tree. I hid behind it, and when he shot, the branches
flew, left and right.

I kept turning, and he was determined to kill me.

So every time he made a circle back—they have to go a little farther to
make the complete turn—

I was hiding, and he came from the other side, until the whole tree was
splintered.

And there was an overpass on the ditch and finally I dashed for it and put
my head in the pipe.

And you know, Pamela, my last thought was,

I've seen so many people killed and dismembered,

and I thought,

"Well, I'll save my head. I'm gone now, for sure. I'll save my head."

And I put it in the pipe so that when people would find me, they would
know who I am.

And with that, the pilot thought that he killed me.

And so all of a sudden someone tugged at me. And I came out and they
said,

"She's alive!"

They had watched this. And I said

"Am I?!"

I remember that. It was clear.

It was Easter morning and we saw eggshells somewhere close by.[11]

Already dis-membered in some sense, separated from her family, friends, and home community—those things that show us who we are—and certain of her own death, Katja's last thought was to preserve her face so that others would see a whole countenance. Even in death, she was determined that she would be known, although she would no longer be able to know herself.

I believe it is significant that in her telling of this experience, Katja recalls that it took place on Easter, the day signified in this story by broken eggshells. In her memory, wholeness and survival are linked with resurrection, the spirit's return to a broken body. The resurrection—which mirrors the miracle of embodiment first enacted in incarnation—made it possible for Jesus to be seen by his grieving friends. Bodily presence and the other's consummation completed the figure of Christ and served as proof of his identity and basis for belief. Klassen notices in Katja's story both the will to keep a physical face intact and a mind working "to piece together a fragmented life" through the telling of story.[12] Both efforts underline the constant task of constructing from shards of experience wholes that can then be shared with, and regarded by, others.

We cannot see ourselves as given or already "consummated," for then we would be static, "finalized," in Bakhtin's word; we would be dead. In order to live, to keep writing the narrative of existence, we must always face a blank page, but we never write by ourselves. Through daily interactions with strangers and those we love, through memory and reflection, we are constantly offered information and images.[13] So for Bakhtin, the command must be "love your neighbor as your neighbor"—as the one beside you whom you have beheld with a benevolent and consummating gaze—and, to the extent that it is possible, "love yourself as your neighbor." Only from the perspective of the other can we come to know the contours of our inner selves or appreciate our own bodies' aesthetic forms. This is why people hire therapists to listen as they construct the stories of their lives. This is why a mirror cannot replace another's gaze.

I think of the first time I modeled for an artist, Cay Lang, a California photographer who had gotten a grant to work for a few days with an enormous Polaroid camera in New York City. For her work, Cay positioned the camera below a large piece of Plexiglas on which she arranged draped human bodies, partly pressed against the surface. When the paper was stripped from the first image of me and the 20 x 24–inch Polaroid image gradually appeared, I was surprised to see a transformed vision of myself that seemed not to be me at all, but some other, lovely woman. That moment had a profound effect on my sense of self. For several years after that I continued to model for artists, unconsciously seeking artful images that would contradict a sense of deficiency and shame, ways to know and appreciate my body differently. Bakhtin describes what happened to me in those events, which granted me another's gift of aesthetic vision: "The profound difference between my inner experience of my own body and the recognition of its outer value by other people—my right to the loving acceptance or recognition of my exterior by others: this recognition or acceptance descends upon me from others like a gift, like grace, which is incapable of being understood and founded from within myself."[14]

Death is a final boundary that contributes to the creation of aesthetic shape. Because our lives begin and end in mystery, our experiences are capable of being aesthetically shaped into stories with beginnings, middles, and endings—but finally not by us. Only another can write the complete text of a life through to its end, interpreting events and giving them meaning after they are completed. It is only near or after the death of someone you love that you can see an entire life and understand its meaning. Though you will never know or account for all the details of a person's biography, your loving attention finds a way

Cay Lang. *Jeanne V.*

to shape those events so that they will remain coherent and significant. Thus, grieving a loss is not only the process of letting go, but it is also the process of keeping, like writing, through acts that allow you to continue to consummate the other. Consider the Jewish practice of sitting shiva—how, for a week after a burial, friends of the deceased gather in his home to share anecdotes from his life, thereby constructing an anthology of shared stories. It may be that, lacking an elaborate theology of an afterlife, Jewish tradition thus ensures the survival of the soul as the living preserve the memory of the dead.

In his essay, Bakhtin mentions the *Paradiso,* wherein Dante asserts that the body will be resurrected after death, "not for its own sake but for the sake of those who knew and loved our one-and-only countenance" in life.[15] In Canto XIV, where disembodied souls of theologians and philosophers are represented as flames or glowing lights, one being expresses his desire for incarnation:

> When our flesh, made glorious at the Judgment Seat,
> > dresses us once again, then shall our persons
> > become more pleasing in being more complete. (43–45)

> But as a coal, in giving off its fire,
> > outshines it by its living incandescence,
> > its form remaining visible and entire;

> so shall this radiance that wraps us round
> > be outshone in appearance by the flesh
> > that lies this long day through beneath the ground; (52–57)

Then the speaker is joined by a chorus of other souls:

> . . . with such prompt zeal as to make evident
> how much they yearned to wear their flesh again;

> perhaps less for themselves than for the love
> > of mothers, fathers, and those each soul held dear
> > before it became an eternal flame above. (62–66)[16]

Even the desire for life after death is fueled more by the love of others than by love of the self. Like Katja, who instinctively shoved her head into a pipe to save her face, these souls long to be recognized by those who knew their names and loved them. And these souls know, as did Job, that they must inhabit bodies in order to see and to be seen by another: "And though worms destroy this body, yet in my flesh shall I see God" (Job 19:26).

Mennonite Aesthetics

For some time I've tried to capture in language what happens when traditional Mennonites sing in four parts, to describe that remarkable quality of passion and joy that makes heavy Anabaptist bodies almost levitate during congregational singing. Once, I speculated that a cappella singing must be a kind of sublimation for passionate but obedient bodies conformed to a narrow range of action and feeling. But it is more than that. In times past, singing was the most common artistic expression permitted in my own Mennonite group.[17] For many years the only permissible form of music was a cappella singing. Maybe singing was permitted because it served worship, but hymn texts must be written at some point, as are some sermons, and Mennonites have published didactic religious materials for centuries.

Unlike imaginative writing, singing uniquely binds people in a shared task and creates an artistic and spiritual event that all can experience at once. Mennonites raised in traditional congregations learn early how to blend their voices in four-part harmony. On a Sunday morning, ordinary homemakers, farmers, and business folk sing with heart-rending clarity and passion. On Sunday evenings, Cambridge intellectuals gathered for worship at the tiny Mennonite fellowship in Sommerville, Massachusetts, sing the old hymns a cappella. At Ohio family reunions, several generations sing together for entire afternoons. As the last note of a hymn barely falls silent, someone calls out the number of the next. During my adolescence, my apparently assimilated Mennonite peers dragged hymnals along on bus trips and campouts so we could practice the most complicated, several-paged arrangements at the back of the hymnal—not unlike our Amish counterparts, whose primary social activity is the hymn sing. I have been at church business meetings fraught with conflict when the suggestion is made to cease speaking and sing, as if this experience will express the underlying intention and experience of community even when consensus seems unlikely, and singing in that case may simply be a tactic to avoid conflict. Singing, a congregation simultaneously produces and consumes an aesthetic whole. Maybe in this, the quintessential communal activity, Mennonites most keenly feel what it is to *be* the Body of Christ.

Singing enables a person to feel deeply connected to others and also to transcend one's own body as well as the mass of the collective group. Rosanna McGonegal Yoder, portrayed as a nineteenth-century Amish adolescent, expresses this contradictory idea in her reflection on the way singing entangles individual ecstasy with community belonging: "My! Isn't it nice just to be alive. Isn't it wonderful to sing like we sang tonight! Why sometimes I felt as if my body was getting so light I couldn't keep my feet on the floor. I thought sometimes the singing would just carry me away! Singing, friends, church, home! Isn't life beautiful!" Even as the aesthetic experience threatens to "carry her away," a progression of "singing, friends, church, home" reflects the complex and powerful construct of human connections that bind Rosanna to earth and to others. Rosanna's fear of flying "away" from her identity groups (friends, church, home) was articulated in a memoir written by her son, J. W. Yoder, whose musical ability, literary authority, and uncharacteristic individualism and ambition carried him to the margins of the Amish-Mennonite community all of his life.[18]

The connective properties of sound must lie at the heart of the Mennonite preference for song: to sing and to hear music implies a chorus or congregation, but to look at an icon or text implies individual perception. *Hearing connects; sight selects.* Or, as Walter Ong in his study of the consequences of literacy puts it, "Sight isolates, sound incorporates." He notes that this principle has special significance in religious practice, where even text-supported Christian traditions such as those in the West continue to privilege the spoken word because of its connective properties. God speaks to us, not writes to us, and we gather to *hear* his word, not to *read* it, because reading individualizes and isolates.[19] I have wondered if my exasperating and very un-Mennonite flat ear has something to do with my becoming a writer. Barely able to sing in tune with the rest of the congregation, I have chosen to work in silence, alone, even as my earliest childhood poems, in subject and form, resembled hymns. I have wondered if implications of the body metaphor—inside is good; outside is bad—make memorized texts and spoken or sung language somehow more precious than written texts because writing, and especially publishing, remove and separate language from the body.

"Mennonite hymns can still make me weep," writes Canadian poet Di Brandt. Her sorrow seems to stem from a sense that the chorus of history and community might easily well up and overpower her own voice. Is it possible, she wonders, both to belong to the chorus (or a collective sectarian silence) and also be a writer, which, by definition, means to speak from a distanced or individual position? Here is her entire prose poem reflecting on this dilemma of Mennonite identity:

> i have tried everything, obedience, disobedience, running away, coming back, forgetting (blanking it out), recalling it again out of the dark, killing it off, translating, leaving it. sometimes it's like a glow running through me, around me, to the horizon like an aura, sometimes it's like a scar, throbbing, on my sleeve. sometimes i visualize it as a suitcase i drag around with me, centuries old, unwieldy, cumbersome, *my people's words,* handcuffing me, binding me, & then again, i open it in a new place & it's filled with colored scarves, playthings. Mennonite hymns can still make me weep. there is so much revisioning i've had to do in order to stay alive: i feel so much anger for the way we were made to suffer, as children, as women, swallowing our desires in secret, submitting to the will of the fathers & God & fate, learning our own silence. i feel so angry when i see Mennonite women trying to forget (blank out) their lives as they grow old, because there was so

much suffering in them, the way they have learned at great cost *not to speak.* sometimes i feel like screaming for them, sometimes i feel like screaming at them. sometimes i long to go back to my grandmother's garden, filled with gooseberries & strawberries & blackberries & crab-apples & rhubarb & red currants & blue currants & raspberries & blackberries, & all the children, aunts & uncles, my family. I hate having to choose between my inherited identity & my life: traditional Mennonite *versus* contemporary Canadian woman writer, yet how can i be both & not fly apart?[20]

The question posed in this prose poem—How can an individual embody all the conflicting identities and images acquired in the course of a life?—is powerfully answered through the consummating force of an aesthetic work. Brandt gives form to the chaos of life; even as she poses the question, she shows her self whole. Though it feels as though she might "fly apart," she won't because she has not sought to suppress any of the dissonant voices within herself, nor has she tried to harmonize them into one. All experience counts; all constituent members speak within a self, even in dissonance. Compare this to the image of the pulverized grains baked to form a single loaf, the grapes crushed to make wine.

Mikhail Bakhtin can speak to Mennonite experience because he directly addressed questions of individual voice in relation to the chorus. He wrote in the wake of the nineteenth-century Slavophile movement, which celebrated traditional Russian culture, rooted in agrarian village life and deep religious belief, even as it was disappearing. According to Emerson, Slavophiles claimed that "'*communality*' made Russian Christians different and better than their isolated, intellectually arrogant Western cohorts"—a boast of superior culture and blood that may not be unfamiliar to some contemporary Anabaptists. While Bakhtin accepted and affirmed the notion of communality from Slavophile religious thought, he saw the chorus as only the beginning. His concern was not how individuals remain part of the chorus, but how the chorus comes to be "individualized" or expressed within each person.[21]

So rather than view the metaphor of communion primarily as the collapse of individual personalities to form one loaf, which represents the Body of Christ, one could place an emphasis on the act of partaking of communion—eating the body of Christ as symbolized by the bread—as a simultaneous partaking of the Body by each individual member. For Mennonites who share my background, the purpose of eating the bread and drinking the wine was therefore not only to imbibe and identify with suffering but also to become united to others and to God in a communion of spirit and flesh so powerful that it collapsed personal boundaries while creating an exclusive edifice. The customs of the Last Supper are the legacy of an embodied God, however, and Christians believe that Jesus shared our gorgeous human form, physically present on earth, in order to perform real acts of love. Following this embodied God, believers would fully inhabit their own bodies and be able to consummate others; formed by a Creator, they would create. In the mystery of the Eucharist, the body of Christ becomes individualized in all who partake of it, so that they may humbly enact works of love in the world.

Humble is a word I find at once familiar and difficult to use, since traditional Anabaptist injunctions to be humble have sometimes served

Albrecht Dürer, *Christ Appears to Mary Magdalene.* With a spade on his shoulder, Jesus is figured as Adam in the iconographic language of Dürer's day, a resurrected Savior sympathetic with the human activities of toil, nurture, and the cycles of nature and mortality.

to silence the voices of many while protecting the authority of a few. Nevertheless, I claim the best kind of humility Mennonite tradition has taught—the kind symbolized by the practice of footwashing, which points as much to the Last Supper as to Mary Magdalene's daring and sensuous demonstration of love: washing her Savior's feet with costly perfume and drying them with her long hair. (Is it any wonder that she was the first to see Jesus embodied after his death?) This kind of humility is characterized by a commitment to listening to others and to serving others. It gives rise to the kind of conversation that has the potential to transform another's life, reconciling a distant individual to himself and to the community rather than angering and alienating him. It is antithetical to pride, which is ultimately the belief that individuals or communities do not need to consider the perspectives of others in order to understand and define themselves.

If boundaries can be seen as limits that give form to all living, changing organisms, then we will honor them because they give aesthetic shape to our lives and the lives of the communities we inhabit. In practices concerning community discipline and membership, relationships between the individual and community may then be cast differently—as mutually defining and mutually consensual, as dynamic and creative—because they are conversational, not coercive. The group would be seen, not as opposed to "the world," but as engaged in loving, form-giving dialogue with it. Outsiders or those who inhabit the margins of the community would be valued for their ability to offer consummating images of the Body in relation to its context, images that are sometimes painful and that are impossible to grasp from an interior perspective. Those in the community who challenge its norms would be valued—more than any writer of policy or theology—as the ones best able to initiate conversations that help to determine the Body's shape.

BROOKLYN, 1996; CAMP HILL, 2000

THE WITNESS A BODY BEARS

What can I do to change my fate
but take a strange lover and cleave
to my work? The Amish believe
it is sinful to be sure
their souls are saved.
The only defense against their worst fears
is work and hope, *Arbeite und Hoffe.*

The work that they mean
darkens your skin with sun
and roughens your hands; you must strain
as a horse against a harness, as light
against the darkness.

Work and Hope

∠⁓

——

7

In Lancaster for the weekend to celebrate Thanksgiving with my family, I was among the first to register at the Mennonite Historical Society Library on Friday morning. I had come to learn whatever I could about the circumstances leading to the translation and printing of the first American edition of *Martyrs Mirror,* a compilation of more than four thousand accounts of people who were baptized as adults, practiced nonresistance, and died for their faith. No book except the Bible has been more important to Mennonite belief and practice.[1] Although it may not be read by many today, this huge book remains an important emblem of Mennonite identity. During 1748–49 the Seventh Day Baptists at Ephrata, Pennsylvania, produced a German edition. I was especially interested in their decision to print an image and motto on the book's title page. The image that captured my imagination was a woodcut of a European peasant digging in a field or vineyard outside a village, beneath the phrase *Arbeite und Hoffe.* The motto, "work and hope," had been familiar to me for some time. In fact, I had already used it in the poem that is partially cited at the beginning of this essay—though as is almost always the case with my knowledge of Mennonite culture, the information had come through conversation, and I knew nothing about the origin of the motto or image.[2]

Articles and books on the publication history of *Martyrs Mirror* offered few clues, yet as I examined the old editions of the book in the Lancaster archives, I discovered that the phrase and/or forms of the picture continued to appear on title pages of all German versions of *Martyrs Mirror* printed in America (and in one English edition) until the image was finally removed with the 1990 printing. In 1996 the image was restored to the German edition as a consequence of my research.

What were the sources of this motto and image? Why did it persist, and how did it evolve during its 330-year printing history? Could I discover any significance that it may have had for the printers at Ephrata and for the Mennonite and Amish publishers who continued to replicate it? Beyond these questions, I wondered what unspoken, unrecognized search for meaning lurked behind my curiosity. In view of the martyr stories, what individual necessity had inspired this quest for the meaning of "work and hope," a search that even I regarded as somewhat arcane?

While I rifled through the card catalogues and browsed through the stacks that morning, my brothers, father, and nephews were mulching the garden and spreading lime on the lawn at my brother's house. This family get-together was another of the sort that prompts disgruntled in-laws to complain, "Why do we travel all this way for everyone to work? Doesn't your family know how to do anything else?" We do sometimes turn gatherings into "frolics," occasions in which toil binds us together in a common task. Sometimes we blame it on our Amish roots or on the Spicher (Speicher) line, which was

 known by some in Mifflin County for being particularly driven to hard work. My grandfather, they say, had his trousers hemmed a couple of inches above his shoes so that they wouldn't get caught in his work and so no one

Ephrata, 1748–49.

would mistake him for an idle man. No doubt my own questions about labor and about what counts as real work first attracted me to the woodcut of that little man with a shovel. As I pursued him, I found it strangely comforting to find him still digging, as I was also digging, each time I lifted the cover of an old leather-bound edition of *Martyrs Mirror* and turned to the title page.[3]

Ephrata Edition — The little man, with an elaborate fraktur on the title page of the Ephrata *Martyrs Mirror,* was probably made from the printer's device on the title page of the 1685 Amsterdam edition. At Ephrata the image was replicated in reverse and in a slightly rougher form, which suggests a derivative copying process such as a woodblock cut directly from an oil-paper tracing of the original. The most striking aspect of the appropriation of the Dutch device by the printers at Ephrata was their decision to translate the Latin motto *Fac et spera* (Do/work and hope) into the German imperative. The choice to translate the motto into the language of the *Martyrs Mirror* text strengthened a connection between the book and the image that may not have persisted if the phrase had remained in its original language. Thus, the act of translation had the effect of incorporating the device into the *Martyrs Mirror* text for most of its German-language publication history in America.

The events preceding an agreement to print *Martyrs Mirror* at Ephrata have been recounted often.[4] Although early Mennonite settlers brought copies of the book from Europe in the late 1600s, comparatively few Pennsylvania Mennonites could read those Dutch editions. As tensions between England and France increased and because the colonial Assembly had refused their appeals for military exemption on religious grounds, the American Mennonite community needed access to the Anabaptist martyr stories as models of resistance to militarism and of submission to the teachings of the religious community. In October 1745, four leaders from the Skippack community in the Franconia area of southeastern Pennsylvania wrote to Mennonites in Amsterdam request-

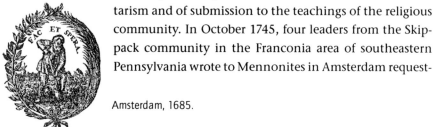

Amsterdam, 1685.

ing help to translate and print a complete German *Martyrs Mirror* for use in the colony:

> As the flames of war appear to mount higher, no man can tell whether the cross and persecution of the defenseless Christians will not soon come, and it is therefore of importance to prepare ourselves for such circumstances with patience and resignation, and to use all available means that encourage steadfastness and strengthen faith. Our whole community has manifested a unanimous desire for a German translation of the *Bloody Theater* *[Martyrs Mirror]* of Thieleman Janz van Braght, especially since in this community there is a very great number of newcomers, for which we consider it to be of greatest importance that they should become acquainted with the trustworthy witnesses who have walked in the way of truth, and sacrificed their lives for it.[5]

The Dutch reply, which arrived nearly three years later, advised the Skippack leaders to translate passages from the book themselves and to get school children to copy them out by hand. Meanwhile, the Pennsylvania Mennonites had already contacted the Seventh Day Baptist community at Ephrata, whose printing press rivaled Benjamin Franklin's.

Mennonites were not strangers to the communitarian group at Ephrata and its charismatic Pietist leader, Conrad Beissel. Before emigrating to America from Germany, Beissel may have encountered Anabaptists during his journeyman travels through southern Germany, when he seemed to learn as much about the contemporary religious underground as he did about his bread baking trade. Certainly after emigrating to Pennsylvania he met Mennonites, who— along with other German-speaking sectarians such as the Amish, Schwenkfelders, Moravians, and Dunkers—shared aspects of his views on Christian pacifism, rejection of loyalty oaths, adult baptism, the community of believers, respect for the land, and separation from "the world." When he first moved west of Germantown, seeking solitude on the Conestoga frontier, Beissel built a cabin about three

miles from a Swiss Mennonite settlement and was probably influenced by their ideas about simplicity of lifestyle and mutual aid.
Mennonites were also among those who came to hear Beissel preach
on the Conestoga, and the *Chronicon Ephratense* notes that by early
1732 Beissel's congregation along Mill Creek was mostly made up
of individuals who had previously been affiliated with Mennonite
groups.[6]

A permanent settlement of Beissel's celibate followers was established along the Cocalico Creek at Ephrata by the mid-1730s, and the
community's printing establishment became the primary source of
religious literature for Mennonites in colonial America. Equipped with
a press and metal type from Germany, and managed by several experienced bookmakers, the printing press came into full production
around 1745. That year saw the completion of a devotional book for
the Mennonites as well as a 120-page collection of stories from *Martyrs
Mirror* under the title *Das Andenken einiger heiligen Martyrer,* which was
probably created as a forerunner of the full-length version completed
in 1748.[7]

The translation of *Martyrs Mirror* began in September 1745, during
one of the most difficult periods of the community's history. Conrad
Beissel had just placed a powerful community leader, Israel Eckerling,
under the ban, and he and his brother Samuel fled Ephrata shortly
thereafter. Two other brothers, Gabriel and Emanuel Eckerling, followed later that year. The Eckerlings had been responsible for devel-
oping a system of mills and workshops at Ephrata, which, combined
with farming and trade activities, had earned the community wealth
and distinction in the colony. During the period when Beissel was
negotiating with the Mennonites to translate and print the large
martyr book, fires consumed the grist, oil, and fulling mills. At the
time, some speculated that Beissel may have started the fires to dimin-
ish the Eckerlings' influence and to purge the community of material-
istic attitudes, but no proof of this remains. Nonetheless, after the
Eckerlings' expulsion, Beissel dismantled the commercial structure

they had created. He dismissed workers hired from outside the community, sold horses and wagons, and refused to take new orders from merchants.[8]

When the mills were rebuilt, concentrated work on the martyr book resumed. The *Chronicon Ephratense* reports that during this period the household of the brothers (the celibate or "solitary" males) was occupied with little else. Fifteen men were assigned to work on the project: nine in the print shop (one translator, four compositors, four pressmen) and six in the paper mill. Consequently, the brethren fell deeply into debt, a humble condition that may have fitted Beissel's vision for a community of faith. Moreover, the enormously demanding task was felt to be a martyrdom for the faithful:

> That this Book of Martyrs was the cause of many trials among the solitary, and contributed not a little to their spiritual martyrdom, is still in fresh remembrance. The Superintendent [Beissel], who started the work, had other reasons than gain for it. Those three years, during which said book was in press, proved an excellent preparation for spiritual martyrdom, although during that time six failed and joined the world again. When this is taken into consideration, as also the low price, and how far those who worked at it were removed from self-interest, the biographies of the holy martyrs, which the book contains, cannot fail to be a source of edification to all who read them.[9]

The entire text was translated from Dutch into German by Peter Miller (Johann Peter Muller, also known in the community as Jaebez and Agrippa), a brilliant German Pietist trained at the University of Heidelberg, who is believed to have been able to read fourteen languages. A visitor to the Ephrata cloister, Israel Acrelius, wrote in his *History of New Sweden* that Miller "labored for three years upon the translation, and was at the same time so burdened with work that he did not sleep more than four hours during the night."[10] Miller's translation was then proofread by Franconia Mennonites Heinrich Funck and Dielman Kolb. Miller may have chosen to translate the Latin motto in consultation with these proofreaders—or possibly

under the influence of Beissel himself. Certainly the motto's sentiments of work and hope expressed Beissel's attitude toward the Eckerling affair and its aftermath. Beissel believed that hard *work* would dis-
pel material security and restore the necessity for spiritual *hope* and
piety:

> The Superintendent [Beissel], who was the instigator of this work, never
> allowed a suspension of work or carnal rest in the settlement, and therefore
> seized every opportunity to keep all those who were under his control in
> perpetual motion, so that no one might ever feel at home again in this life,
> and so forget the consolation from above, which purpose this Book of Mar-
> tyrs excellently served.[11]

European Origins

The image printed on the title page of the Ephrata edition—though derived from the 1685 Amsterdam *Martyrs
Mirror*—can be traced to the book's first printing, in 1660,
by Jacob Braat of Dordrecht. The title page of the 1660 edition bears
an elaborate colophon, or emblem, in which a divine arm extends a
laurel wreath to reward the peasant who labors outside the village
under the motto *Fac et spera*. Braat also used a simpler version of the
device for smaller volumes, such as Adriaen van Nispens's *Verscheyde
Voyagien,* a compilation of travel writings printed in Dordrecht in
1652. A copy of this tiny book, which I found in the New York Public
Library, rested easily in the palm of my hand. The printer's device,
which appears six times in one of two sizes on various title pages
throughout the volume, consists only of the central oval encompass-
ing the digging peasant. A tetragrammaton is inscribed amidst radiant
beams above his head, the unpronounceable name of God replacing
the divine arm of the more elaborate version.

Dordrecht, 1660.

From *Verscheyde Voyagien, ofte rysen . . .*
(Dordrecht, 1652).

Printer's device of Gellius Ctemantius
(1554–1602).

Briels's directory of sixteenth- and seventeenth-century Dutch printers and booksellers shows both forms of the device and attributes them to Jacob Braat (Braet), who was active as a printer in Dordrecht from c. 1643 to 1665 and in Utrecht in 1652.[12] This device may be related to one used by Gellius Ctemantius (Gilles van der Erve). This image illustrates Matthew 13:44, which encircles it: Het rike der hemelen is als een verborgen schat in den acker (The kingdom of heaven is like a treasure hidden in a field). The following verse continues, "When a man found it, he hid it again, and then in his joy went and sold all he had and bought that field" (NIV). It would seem, then, that this image portrays the man, leaning on his shovel, in the midst of the transaction that will purchase the field containing a secret treasure. Curiously, we see a digger at work behind the man. He is either hiding the treasure from the field's original owner or searching for more. The stance and costume of this small figure so closely match the digger of Braat's device that it seems he may have been the original model. In light of this origin, the work of the digger may have had a more specific meaning, at least for Braat: the kingdom of heaven is worthy of the all-consuming, all-demanding labor required to establish it on earth. Braat chose to combine the image with a less specific text: *Fac et spera.*

This motto is listed in another directory in connection with six additional European printers active between 1625 and 1687. Their locations, scattered from Rouen to Leipzig—and the absence of Braat's name from this list—suggest that other printers may have used the motto as well.[13] The Latin phrase is likely derived from St. Jerome's Vulgate translation of the Bible: Spera in domino et fac bonitatem et inhabita terram et pasceris in diuitiis eius (Trust in the Lord and do good; so you will dwell in the land, and enjoy security. Psalm 37:3, RSV).[14] Briels lists Braat's second address as "In de Werkende Hoop" (at the sign of the working hope), suggesting that the image of a digging man may have been on the trade sign that hung outside his print shop.

A man digging with a shovel is certainly not an unusual image for that time; art historian Raimond Van Marle notes that Italian artists of the fifteenth century particularly favored this figure, as is evident in miniatures and sketch albums from that period. From ancient Roman times and throughout the Early Christian, Carolingian, and Romanesque periods, images of peasants engaged in realistic, concrete tasks were used to signify seasons and months. The succession of the peasants' toil served as an allegory of a larger order, and throughout the Middle Ages, agricultural work was depicted in miniature on manuscripts and borders of calendars. In some Romanesque and Gothic churches, reliefs portraying peasants at work were paired with signs of the Zodiac.[15] At the cathedral of Amiens, for instance, the image of a man digging at the base of a vine serves as a symbol for the month of March. Other examples of "the works and days" series can be found on the campanile of Florence, probably sculpted from a drawing by Giotto, at the Church of San Petronio in Bologna and on the ceiling above the altar at Salisbury Cathedral in England. More recently, a

Symbol of the month of March drawn by Darcy Lynn from a photograph of a calendar relief on the cathedral at Amiens.

Almanac illustration for the month of March.

peasant digging under the sign of Aries appears in the March section of the 1839 almanac produced by an Amish-Mennonite Frenchman, *L'Anabaptiste ou le Cultivateur par Expérience.*

Explaining the presence of agricultural images in religious art—where laboring peasants often appear beside saints—Emil Male writes, "The primeval work of tilling the soil, the task which God Himself imposed on Adam . . . the Church seems to have given foremost place."[16] That peasants and farmers extend the work of Adam seems obvious, but that the little digging man on Jacob Braat's printer's device represents Adam—or that he was read as representing Adam *at one time*—seems less certain. Yet, in his massive study of the iconography of secular art in Medieval and Renaissance times, Van Marle concludes that the image of a digging man originates with, *and refers to,* the iconography of Adam after the Fall. To support this claim, Van Marle cites numerous examples of the figure that appear in European Christian manuscripts and decorative art.[17]

Anabaptists likely recognized Adam in the woodblock illustration from the 1692 Dutch edition of Schabaelje's *The Wandering Soul,* long since a favorite of Mennonite readers. In one episode of the story,

Adam

Felipe Gauman
Pomo de Ayala, "The
First World: Adam
and Eve."

this Adam, who bears an uncanny resemblance to the man on Braat's device, explains his life sentence of labor as symbolized by the shovel.[18]

The digging Adam also traveled to the New World with Spanish explorers and appears in a 1613 manuscript written in Spanish and Quechua by an Andean worker in the colonial government of Peru. His letter addressed to the King of Spain, called *The First New Chronicle and Good Government,* included 800 pages of text and 400 line drawings that tell the history of the Christian world from an American Indian viewpoint. In a spirit of cultural hybridity that printers of *Martyrs Mirror* in Anglo-America would also employ, the artist replaced Adam's shovel with a native American digging stick and situated him under the sun, while Eve sits beneath the moon, in keeping with Andean spatial symbolism.[19]

Back in Europe, the process of adapting the Dordrecht printer's device began with the second edition of *Martyrs Mirror,* printed in 1685. It is not known why the Amsterdam printers borrowed and redrew Braat's insignia, although Joseph Springer, curator of the Mennonite Historical Library at Goshen College, speculates that they may have wished to claim a connection between this book and the first edition.[20] By 1685 Thieleman van Braght, the original author and compiler, was already dead, and the new edition had been revised by anonymous editors. Although referring to the simpler form of Braat's device, the image used at Amsterdam does differ significantly: the tetragrammaton and radiant lines above the digger's head are absent, and a cross is added to the church steeple in the village to signify divine presence. A bird perched on the vine—not present in the larger colophon of the 1660 edition—refers to the Holy Spirit appearing in the form of a dove at Christ's baptism and also to the dove that returned to Noah's ark as a symbol of hope and God's faithfulness. Except for the deviant 1814–15 version noted below, the bird appears in all subsequent interpretations of the image. The association between the book and the device that began in Amsterdam persisted only in America, for when Mennonites in Pirmasens (Palatinate) issued a copy of the Ephrata *Martyrs Mirror* in 1780, they used a rather nondescript floral ornament without a motto on the title page.

American Adaptations

A most extraordinary translation of the Ephrata device appeared on the title page of a new German edition of the book published during 1814–15 by Joseph Ehrenfried of Lancaster, Pennsylvania. This digger—two generations removed from the peasant on Braat's trademark—has clearly migrated from Europe to the American frontier. Clothed in colonial costume, he spades a field near a small herd of sheep and a thatch-roofed home with an attached stable. There is no sign of a village or community nearby; this settler is part of a new agricultural system based on individual ownership of private property that will not include the European village. It may be that this image was a stock engraving of the time to which the motto *Arbeite und Hoffe* was simply added, although the uncanny relationship between this and earlier versions of the image suggests a conscious transformation.

Twenty-four years later, in 1837, the first English edition of *Martyrs Mirror*, translated by Isaac D. Rupp, was published in Lancaster County. On the lower half of its title page, in the printer's mark position, the motto *Arbeite und Hoffe* starkly appears between two thin lines—the

Lancaster, Pa., 1814.

only German words on the page. In a curious reversal of the Ephrata decision to translate a Latin motto into the language of the text, Rupp, or perhaps David Miller, the publisher, chose to include the motto but not to translate it—as though it carried special meaning in German that could not transcend transformation into the public language of government and commerce. Like the persistence of Pennsylvania German words in the vocabulary of English-speaking Mennonites today, this phrase points to a prior, favored way of thinking and naming the world. English eventually replaced German and Pennsylvania German in Mennonite domestic and religious discourse, and all later English editions of *Martyrs Mirror* failed to use the *Arbeite und Hoffe* motto or device. What might have happened if Rupp had chosen to keep the image and translate the motto into the language of the text, as was done at Ephrata? One can only speculate about whether "Work and Hope" and the little man with the shovel might have remained part of the text, still with us on the title page of the 1886 Joseph Sohm English translation in use today.

In 1849 Shem Zook, an Amish-Mennonite from Mifflin County, Pennsylvania, revised the German *Martyrs Mirror* and had it printed in Philadelphia. The title page of this edition bears an elegant new device apparently copied from the 1748 edition. This image retains the reversed orientation of Ephrata, and the digger, who seems to have aged, wears the original European peasant's costume. The palm and olive branches are more florid, and the vine has grown into a stumpy tree. A horizon line above the digger's head suggests the low mountains that are always within sight in Zook's native Kishacoquillas Valley, and a steepled church and several buildings cluster at the foot of the mountain. The steeple cross, obvious in the 1685 Dutch device and less apparent in the Ephrata edition, is gone from Zook's version altogether, perhaps in keeping with Amish-Mennonite plain style.

Of course, Mennonites of this period did not build steeples on their meetinghouses either—a point not lost on John F. Funk, who published another German edition

Philadelphia, 1849.

at Elkhart, Indiana, in 1870. The device on his title page is nearly identical to the Zook edition, except that the steepled church is replaced by a single-story building more consistent with the architecture of Mennonite meetinghouses. A sample book of the engravings used by John Funk, now housed in the Mennonite Historical Library collection at Goshen, Indiana, contains two versions of the device: one with the motto and one without. Since Funk cut two engravings, he must have considered eliminating the motto but finally chose to keep it. Funk's image remained on the subsequent German printings of *Martyrs Mirror* published at Scottdale, Pennsylvania; Berne, Indiana; and Aylmer, Ontario.

Pathway Publishers, an Amish establishment in Canada, removed the image from its 1990 printing, replacing it with one of the Jan van Lyken engravings created to illustrate the 1685 Dutch edition. David Luthy, writer, publisher, and director of the Heritage Historical Library at Aylmer, claimed responsibility for the decision: "I alone get credit or discredit for that! I am a big Dirk Willems (martyr of 1569) fan and decided to put him on the title page. I have said to people that the poor man with the shovel has been digging long enough. So, you see, I have in a way tampered with history, but we know who Dirk was and the other man was fictional yet symbolic."[21] Choosing a representative illustration over a symbol is consistent with Amish values of tradition, simplicity, and factual accounts over fiction. Indeed, Luthy believes that the image was previously retained "simply because it was always there." He adds that "not a single person ever mentioned to us that they miss it from the title page." As a result of the research reported in this article, however, Luthy restored the image to the title page of the 1996 edition.

It would be difficult to determine whether the *Arbeite und Hoffe* motto and symbol express North American Amish or Mennonite beliefs, although there is evidence of its use in other contexts. In the Ohio Mennonite communities settled mostly by nineteenth-century Swiss immigrants, for in-

Elkhart, Ind., 1870.

stance, the motto persisted through the custom of painting text on barns. The east side of the Peter Schumacher barn, located between Pandora and Bluffton, Ohio, bore the rhyme *An Gottes Segen ist alles gelegen* (everything depends on God's blessing), while the other end of the barn read *Arbeite und Hoffe.* The pairing of these two mottoes on a barn—the storage place of grain, hay, and implements; shelter for livestock; and center of the agricultural enterprise—suggests that human labor and hope, although necessary, do not ultimately ensure prosperity without God's blessing.[22]

In another instance, the image was interpreted and reproduced on the cover of *The Diary,* a newsletter "dedicated to the preservation of fundamental movements . . . as well as Old Order religious literature and its virtues," published by Joseph F. Beiler of Gordonville, Pennsylvania. Beneath the device, he printed the lyrics of a nineteenth-century Amish song that begins: "Schaffet, schaffet, Menschenkinder / Schaffet eure Seligkeit" (Work, work children of men / work out your salvation). An editor's note explains that the emblem, affixed to the German *Martyrs Mirror* since 1748, "represents a Christian's effort without ceasing."[23] What does the little man hope for? Might his effort be connected with a desire for eternal life, as my poem suggests?

The theme of working and hoping does emerge in Old Order arguments against the doctrine of assurance of salvation. Former Amishman, John R. Renno, writes that "they argued that we must just do as good as we know how and obey our spiritual leaders, and hope for heaven, hope that the Lord will look at all our honest efforts and that we tried to do right and we were obedient to our preachers, and if that did not reach, he would supply the Grace to get us into heaven at last, once we die." During the 1950s, Renno was excommunicated from the Peachey Amish Church in Mifflin County because he refused to denounce his commitment to this troublesome "Mennonite doctrine." Instead of "assurance of salvation," the Amish believe in a "living hope," explains Luthy in a letter, and "the theology of working and hoping"—that works must accompany faith—is an important

BOUSTROPHEDON

> an ancient mode of writing in which lines
> run alternately from right to left and from
> left to right. Greek: as the ox turns (in plow-
> ing)

A little boy walks behind the plow
picking up stones in a field.
He drops them onto a pile
at the end of the row.
One day these stones will make
a home for his soul. He doesn't know

this yet. How can he know
the meaning of all that the plow
inscribes: that he'll grow to make
a life from this field,
that its meanings will pile
like paint, which he'll stroke in rows,

each dab a seed in a furrow?
He'll have to leave to finally know
all that's concealed in this pile
of limestones. Rocks struck open by
        the plow
reveal the spiral fossils of the field.
Maybe whatever anyone can make

of himself was already made
long ago, order and disorder set in the rows
of a double helix. Settlers clearing fields
often spared single oaks, though they knew
whoever followed would have to plow
around them. Saved from the woodpile,

the trees grow elegant alone and drop piles
of acorns into the troughs that furrows
        make.

Some sprout, but the certain plow
turns saplings under as it carves rows
for corn. In winter, stubble slants in snow
like runes scrawled across the field.

A farmer's son who takes canvas for his field
aches to become an artist, compiles
another family, moves to a city. No
one back home sees or knows what he
        makes:
the way light shifts on those scarred rows
of pigment, though he paints as they plow.

It only takes one person plowing a row
to make a field, then others can follow
knowing they aren't the first or alone.

part of Amish belief. He adds that "while the theology of 'working and hoping' is central to Amish theology, the [*Martyrs Mirror*] device isn't."[24]

Because references to the fruits of labor abound in traditional expressions, it may be best to consider a less specific sense of work's reward in regard to this image. In his writings published during the first half of this century, Joseph W. Yoder repeatedly mentions the importance of work in Amish and Amish-Mennonite culture, especially physical labor on the land. One of his early Pennsylvania German poems, "Noch Denke," reads, "Mir misse all angeh un schaffe, / Und hoffe fur en gutes Glück," which he translated as, "We must all go on and work, / And hope for the best of luck."[25] Apparently, the worker hopes, not for personal salvation or eternal life in heaven, but for a more general sense of well-being on earth: blessing, luck, or, as the *New International Version* renders Psalm 37:3, "safe pasture."

While driving through Lancaster County, Mennonite sociologist Calvin Redekop observes an attempt to create that safe pasture in the large Amish and Mennonite farmsteads, which he regards as an "overcompensation for homelessness in times past."[26] He has attributed Mennonite economic success in farming, not to the "Protestant work ethic" expressed through a "calling," but to other factors, including a desire to gain acceptance and tolerance from landowners and civil authorities. For outsiders, work is one way to overcome a sense of dislocation and achieve security; and American Anabaptists, who seem to value hard work at least as much as they value good works, are not alone in doing so. Exploring the history of cultural outsiders in Europe, French linguist and theorist Julia Kristeva has noted that aliens are workers; it is the foreigners in European society who still value hard work. They "experience an acute pleasure in asserting themselves in and through work: as if *it* [work] were the chosen soil, the only source of possible success, and above all the personal, steadfast, nontransferable quality, but fit to be moved beyond borders and properties."[27] Hence, work becomes both a home and the means of achieving the security of home.

Of course, the foreigner's diligence is often resented by native neighbors. In a French village, Kristeva found that farmers who had moved from another region were "hated as much for being intruders as being relentless." This is a familiar story. In it are echoes of Benjamin Franklin's disgust with the German-speaking settlers in Pennsylvania, whom he described as people who "under-live and are thereby enabled to under-work and under-sell the English."[28] A little Adam—the first outcast of Eden and father of us all—seems an apt expression of the laboring outsider, particularly as it appears in a collection of stories about religious intolerance and persecution.

Although David Luthy wrote with irony that "the poor man with the shovel has been digging long enough," he may be correct—at least if we read the digger as an Anabaptist outsider whose labor is aimed at gaining the acceptance of literal landlords and authorities. These days, county agents boast of the success of the "plain people," whose farming practices, simple lifestyle, and large working families allow them to prosper while others fail. A *New York Times* article reports that "while farmland lies fallow in much of rural New York, an influx of Mennonite families is making agriculture a viable way of life once more." Horning Mennonites from Pennsylvania who moved to upstate New York have revived poor farms through the use of tile drainage, lime, and crop rotation, according to an agent of the Cornell University Cooperative Extension quoted in the article.[29] The "plain people" or most traditional members of the Anabaptist community— Beachy Amish, Holdeman Mennonite, Hutterian Brethren, Old Order Amish, and Old Order Mennonites—are now the fastest growing segment of the Mennonite family and perhaps the most secure on the

New York City–based artist Jerry Kearns knew nothing of the traditional sign when he chose to use a 1950s cartoon image of a female in high heels digging against an urban backdrop. This figure, he said, seemed to express contemporary discussions about affirmative action policy and America's shift from an industrial to a service economy, which is more dependent on women's lower-paying work. The outsider—represented here as female and agrarian—labors where she may feel alien and unwelcome. Jerry Kearns. *Affirmative Action* (1987).

land.[30] As their numbers grow, new groups move into areas where real estate is inexpensive and no longer profitable for others to farm. They work in the tradition of the Anabaptist agriculturists, who, driven from their homes into European hinterlands, devised new farming methods for previously unproductive mountain soil. Or they work in the tradition of their colonial American forebears who settled territories previously occupied by another people whose way of life was endangered and ultimately destroyed.

I find it interesting that the Amish people who retained the German text of *Martyrs Mirror* finally found no need for the little man with the shovel and removed him at precisely the time when the Mennonite Historians of Eastern Pennsylvania chose to resurrect him. Explained John Ruth, who was largely responsible for this decision, "We [Mennonites] have a paucity of images that can go back into history and that are still accessible. This is a venerable thing—it has made the transition from Dutch to German to English."[31]

In 1990, Allan Eitzen was commissioned to update the image. Now part of a permanent exhibit titled "Work and Hope" at The Mennonite Heritage Center in Harleysville, Pennsylvania, the stylized adaptation by Eitzen takes into account previous versions. Although the wreath is oriented like the Ephrata reversal (olive branches on the right, palm on the left), the peasant digs in the direction of the original Dutch version, facing east, facing Europe. Neither of the buildings behind him appears to be a house of worship; instead, they resemble the two-story farm home and springhouse or *daadi-haus* configurations common to eastern Pennsylvania farmsteads. These are the kinds of buildings that are now being razed or saved to anchor new housing developments in that area, which serves as a suburb of Philadelphia.

Perhaps the image of the little man with a shovel has become most useful to American Anabaptists such as me, who have wandered from their homesteads and no longer live by labor on the land. In Brooklyn, downstate from the new community of Horning Mennonites, I was drawn to the one who toils

"Work and Hope" by Allan Eitzen.

From Track Work
poster.

alone outside the walls of the village as I—a woman who wonders if she writes like a Mennonite—tried to make my way through a doctoral program in a city university. Like me, that peasant is tilling fields that may not belong to him yet—working and hoping—not sure if he is entitled to safe pasture in that territory. He labors in silence and solitude as I do most of the time, sometimes plagued by a recognition that I belong to a generation that has exchanged traditional roles and community ties for education and cultural assimilation. Perhaps I am like the assimilated Jewish person, whom Isaac Bashevis Singer describes as "the salt of humanity with his tremendous energy and ambition." Nevertheless, he warns that "being salt, he gives humanity high blood pressure. He's neither a real Jew nor a real Gentile. He has no roots in any group. He digs all the time in other people's soil, but he never reaches any roots."[32]

Yet each time I see that digging man embodied in another form—on the Metropolitan Transit Authority's announcement of subway trackwork, for instance—I feel a flush of nostalgic recognition, connection, and hope. The Anabaptist Adam continued to be reborn because people continued to carry him with them, the work of remembering at least as worthy as working the earth.

When I was on the planning committee for "Quiet in the Land?" the 1995 conference devoted to Anabaptist women's history that was held at Millersville University, I suggested that we use the old printer's mark as an emblem for the event. Other committee members were quick to point out that the digger is male, hardly a fitting image for

Anna Baptist designed by Julie Musselman for a poster and T-shirt.

T-shirts at a conference exploring women's experience. So I asked my friend Julie Musselman, a fashion designer and native daughter of the community that commissioned the original Ephrata *Martyrs Mirror,* to adapt the figure from the 1849 Shem Zook design. In keeping with tradition, we translated the motto as well. After all those years, the Anabaptist Adam had been replaced by an English-speaking Mennonite sister—dressed in a head covering, long-sleeved cape dress, and apron—who seems to be wielding her spade with capable, if grim, determination.

When I got my first full-time academic appointment, I hung a large, framed version of the 1995 female digger in my office, but after a couple of years of laboring in that Anabaptist-affiliated institution, I removed it, needing no reminder to attend to my work. Imagine my surprise a few years later when Adriaan Plak, librarian from the University of Amsterdam, sent a copy of the digger's ancestor depicted on a device from a 1640 catechism prepared by a printer who worked for Mennonites and Remonstrants. Our European foremother, laboring under the tetragrammaton, looks more like a version of Delacroix's "Liberty Leading the People," with her skirt flung open over a muscular thigh, her shapely, low-cut bodice, bare feet, and cap strings or tresses blowing freely in the wind. More gratifying to me than an affirmation of duty or of the mind-numbing drive to work that can sometimes make a human being feel like a mule is this image that seems to express both freedom and focus on her task.[33]

Perhaps I should tell one last story associated with the motto. During the early 1990s my mother's cousin, Leonard Byler, a physician who grew up on a Mifflin County farm, posted this tale on Mennolink, the electronic mail listserv. Len had seen my poem "Freindschaft" in a copy of the *New Yorker* that arrived at his office in Seattle, and on a chalkboard behind his desk scribbled the familiar phrase

Arbeite und Hoffe for his own contemplation. Later that day he was scheduled to meet with the elderly wife of a German immigrant to explain the steps of her husband's leu-

From *Onderwysinge in de Christelijcke . . .*
(Hoorn, 1640).

kemia treatment. He had known the couple for some years and was himself saddened by the news. He writes, "As we talked, her teary eyes caught the words on the chalkboard and she reached for my hand and sobbed, 'Yes, yes, that's all we have isn't it—work and hope!'" The doctor could not bring himself to explain that the phrase had not been placed there for her benefit.[34]

BROOKLYN, 1995; CAMP HILL, 1999

Marilyn, H. S. Bender, and Me

8 One October, on a chilly, gray afternoon of the sort that sometimes lingers in northern Indiana, Canadian novelist Rudy Wiebe and I walked out of a classroom at Goshen College, crossed South Main, and passed the oversized mailbox bearing H. S. Bender's name in plain black-and-white letters. Stark and quite strange, given the fact that the Old Mennonite churchman had been dead for thirty-five years. What a powerful author, we joked. Who still sends letters to H. S. Bender? To whom does he still write?

Then, as if out of nowhere, Rudy said, "I think I first heard about Marilyn Monroe's suicide from H. S. Bender. He announced it at the 1962 Mennonite World Conference in Kitchener—that must have been the first time most people in the audience heard, unless they'd turned on a radio that Sunday morning."

Although he died a few months before I was born, H. S. Bender looms large in my imagination, persistent as his name on that mailbox: father of Mennonite studies, intellectual heavyweight in a dark, plain suit tailored in Lancaster County, Pennsylvania. I see him surrounded by officers of the Mennonite Historical Society in the photograph taken in Goshen sometime during the 1943–44 academic year—the year Bender's "Anabaptist Vision" and Guy F. Hershberger's *War, Peace, and Nonresistance* appeared—at the height of America's involvement in World War II. Of the five somber, dark-suited men in that photo, only ex-Amishman John Umble smiles a little and does not wear the regulation uniform. (Presumably he had his fill of lapel-less jackets growing up.) Front and center, Bender, the benevolent commander-in-chief, sits behind a huge, thickly bound book spread open on a library table. Is that an old leather-bound edition of the *Martyrs Mirror*? Likely. In the battle against cultural assimilation and American militarism, this compilation of persecution and martyrdom served as a model of conscience and sacrifice.[1] Bender worked tirelessly to preserve and promote a scholarly vision of history that would remind Mennonites of a time when their Anabaptist ancestors were willing to lose their lives for the ideological trinity I memorized in a Goshen College classroom: discipleship (the primacy of actions over faith or creed), brotherhood (a covenant community), and nonresistance (pacifism). Bookshelves enclosed in glass behind the men's shoulders suggest that there are many volumes left to read and write. From the look on Bender's face, the weight of that work hangs heavy.

But Bender and Marilyn Monroe? She did carry collections of contemporary poetry and bulky literary classics onto movie sets in a vain attempt to convince journalists and coworkers that, in the words of one movie magazine, "her golden head on her well-formed shoulders was filled with more than 'pink dreams.'"[2] By all accounts she actually read those books and was smarter than she seemed, but we don't remember her for that. Reporters called her marriage to playwright Arthur Miller, "Beauty and the Brain."

No one remembers the photograph of her, curled up in a pair of capri pants and a sleeveless T-shirt, reading James Joyce's *Ulysses*. We remember that famous shot taken in pre-dawn darkness on the set of *The Seven Year Itch*. It's August in that film, and New York City swelters with temptation as a dutiful and bungling businessman, left to work

Officers of the Mennonite Historical Society, 1943–1944, the year of Bender's
Anabaptist Vision. Left to right: S. C. Yoder, John S. Umble, H. S. Bender,
J. C. Wenger, Guy F. Hershberger

in the city while his wife and children vacation upstate, is nearly undone by a blond bombshell who lives in his building. Tom Ewell is
dwarfed by the force of her allure in the poster that advertised the
movie. In our memory, Marilyn stands forever on a grate in the sidewalk as gusts from the subway blow her skirts. Blond Marilyn in a white
halter dress, shameless and bright as an angel, illuminated by the
desire of all of postwar America, demonstrates one way a female could
wield power in a culture that was feeling anxious about the place and
role of men's and women's bodies. Her divorce from celebrity center
fielder Joe Dimaggio would later be traced to her spontaneous episode
of exhibitionism on a subway grate, shot in the wee hours before dawn.

"I've never quite understood this sex symbol business," Marilyn
once said, "but if I'm going to be a symbol of something, I'd rather
have it [be] sex than some other things they've got symbols for."[3]

I now have reason to believe that H. S. Bender did not announce
Marilyn Monroe's suicide, but the image is striking, and its mythic
possibilities persist.[4] How to reconcile those symbols: Bender in black,
Marilyn in white; a man of the book, a woman reduced to the body—

Marilyn Monroe and Tom Ewell in *The Seven Year Itch.*

which was aligned with some of the most powerful men of her day. Mennonite intellectual authority and female allure. Perhaps these figures are no more incongruous than many of the things I encountered growing up in the 1970s in the United States in the Mennonite Church. Yet these especially fascinate me, and I take 1962—the year of my birth—as a lens through which to view changes in Mennonite culture that would shape my own constructs of authority and gender. So that afternoon in Goshen, I pestered Rudy with questions. Of all things, for instance, why did he remember *that*?

Mostly it had to do with larger-than-life Bender, whom Rudy had admired since 1957, when someone gave him a copy of "The Anabaptist Vision," Bender's seminal articulation of Mennonite theology and identity. At the time, Rudy was studying literature at the University at Tübingen, where Bender had done pioneering research on Anabaptism during the 1920s.

The seventh Mennonite World Conference, held during the first week of August in 1962, was Bender's conference: he was its president and planner. Ill health had kept him in Goshen until the conference's final days, however. Someone else read his keynote address, and although he presided over several sessions, he frequently retreated from the platform to rest. When he finally preached to a crowd of 12,000 on Sunday evening, his words carried a particular gravity. In little more than a month, he would be dead from pancreatic cancer.

At the beginning of his sermon, Bender was said to have announced Marilyn's death in an aside that Rudy recalls as not uncharitable but something along these lines: that Marilyn Monroe would die of an overdose of sleeping pills shows that, even among the beautiful and powerful of "the world," there is pain and suffering. "The world" is full of this kind of thing.

Was Bender, himself a public figure full of physical pain and suffering, admitting a sympathetic identification with Marilyn in the sermon that marked the culmination of his career? Probably not. To begin with, there was the problem of her appearance. Although he regarded his own regulation suit as mere cultural artifact and as a concession to eastern Mennonites, Bender admitted biblical support for nonconformed (plain) dress codes for women.[5] A scantily clad, bob-haired female celebrity was a fallen angel from the world outside a community shaped by nonconformity, simplicity, and separation. As Russia embodied evil for a Cold War, presumably Christian nation, so Marilyn served a symbolic and oppositional—if not cautionary—

Movie poster.

function in relation to the Anabaptist-Mennonite community. She represented all that plain Mennonite women were not supposed to be: glamorous, public, exhibitionistic, hedonistic, and promiscuous.

The rest of the sermon advanced Bender's vision for a Mennonite World Conference that had little to do with "the world" at all. Essentially a program of identity fortification and consolidation, the conference aimed to build ties between Mennonites by renewing spiritual life and fostering an appreciation for history. For spiritual revival, there were five different Bible studies to choose from most mornings—two in German and three in English. To promulgate the historic faith, European academics presented papers that prompted one school teacher from British Columbia to remark, "I suspect many people did not have to duck to allow the . . . scholarly dissertations to go over their heads."[6]

Bender had earlier outlined the religious community's proper relation to "the world" in a 1945 conference paper delivered at Goshen: unlike Calvinists and Catholics, Mennonites do not believe that we can redeem creation. Yet, unlike Lutherans and Christian fundamentalists, Mennonites believe that it *is* possible to carry out God's will in a fallen world. It is only possible to establish the kingdom of God on earth within the bounds of a peaceable Christian community. Given the alarming number of Mennonite men who had opted for some form of military service during World War II, and heeding predictions that the church would not survive a migration off the land, Bender believed that the best site for that community was the country village.

In deeply rooted rural communities, traditional patterns of family life and religion felt more secure. Men's bodies had a distinct usefulness in agricultural labor as did women's bodies—in rearing helpers and working as partners on the family farm. A nonprofessional congregation was more likely to support the authoritarian and patriarchal leadership structures that had solidified during the early twentieth century, and a geographically compact agrarian community was more likely to remain isolated from mainstream society. Its distinctive physical marks of religious piety signaled separation even to non-

Mennonite neighbors—whether those marks were the German dialect spoken by many Canadians who attended the Kitchener Mennonite World Conference or the articles of plain dress worn by most of the Americans in that audience. By 1962, however, the rural community, with its separate patterns of life that were nonconformed to the ways of the broader society, no longer captured all of the American Mennonite experience.

Consider another story from that first week of August 1962. A phone rings in a tiny upstairs apartment of a Richmond, Virginia, row house. My mother, twenty-four years old and five months pregnant, will answer it. In this blistering Southern city, she works as a nurse in the Negro wards to support her husband's studies. She is married to a man she has known since she was a girl in braids and he was a barefoot Amish boy in Mifflin County, Pennsylvania. They both attended a Mennonite high school founded after the war as a hedge against cultural assimilation. When they married in 1959, she carried a worldly dozen red roses, one of the first brides at Locust Grove Conservative Conference Mennonite Church to wear a stylish, albeit homemade, floor-length gown. The wedding was so large that, defying the bishop's wishes, the reception was held in a secular community hall rather than in the church basement—which may be one reason that the bishop, who was also the bride's uncle, dropped over dead before the cake was cut.

Now, on the phone, my mother's aunt tearfully says that Vesta, my mother's mother, has also died without warning. Vesta, the articulate and heroic oldest sister, graduated from public high school and displayed her framed diploma in the kitchen of her farm house. She sometimes published her own poems and drawings in *Locust Grove Leaves,* the purple mimeographed newsletter that she edited at church. Bishop Peachey, her brother-in-law, could preach about the immodesty of open-toed shoes and bandanas worn too far back on the hair, and Vesta went along with it, but only—in her words—"to keep the peace." She wore a head covering or bonnet every day, but what people remember is her generosity and artful flower beds. In a highly stratified community, she was kind to people at any place on the plain/fancy continuum, always generous with conversation and coffee. When she felt overwhelmed, the doctor prescribed phenobarbital—"nerve pills"—until her heart gave out at age forty-eight.

When I ask my mother what she remembers about August 1962, she says, "Oh, it was hot. I was pregnant with you. My mother died. Marilyn Monroe died . . ." Only ten years younger than my grandmother, Marilyn was addicted to sleeping pills. My grandmother took "nerve pills." Were all the women, plain or fancy, sedated back then? In 1962, attempting to name whatever was making middle-class American housewives feel mentally numb and complacent, Betty Friedan published in *Mademoiselle* magazine an article that would eventually become *The Feminine Mystique.* The postwar domestication and infantilization of a certain class of white American women she called "the problem that has no name." She blamed the wars, especially the Korean war, for a massive emotional exhaustion that caused both men and women to seek refuge in the image of a nurturing wife-mother within a stable home. (That desire remains in the era of Martha Stewart.) But my mother is already onto her story's next turn.

After she hung up the phone, Mom took her head covering from the dresser top, pinned it to her bun, and kneeled to pray at the bed. Then she grabbed her purse and, doubtless in shock, walked down a sweltering sidewalk to the bank to withdraw some cash for the trip north. Counting out her bills, the teller intoned in a thick southern drawl, "My, that's a lovely net hat you're wearing. Perfectly light for this weather." My mother's hand instantly flew to the prayer veil she'd forgotten to remove. To her, it had never been an article of fashion: a symbol of female subordination and obedience, perhaps, or, for the high-minded gentlemen at Goshen, a sign of Anabaptism's ideals conveniently reserved for the gentler sex. Away from the symbols and codes of her home community, however, and outside the private domain of her urban apartment, the head covering signified nothing except curious style. Eventually, she stopped wearing it for this reason.

At the Kitchener World Conference, even some Mennonites—

AUGUST

Dad's mother was coming home
from picking huckleberries on the mountain
when sunlight spooked the horse, and it tore
through a pasture fence, dragging the buggy
until it broke loose, hurling the children,
killing their mother, spilling
those silver pails of sweet, black fruit.
Mom's mother, just forty-five and already a grandma,
was walking the hill to Locust Grove Church
when she clutched the bodice of her Sunday dress
and slumped to the berm, just past grandpa's silo
filled with the summer's rotting fodder.
And this stepmother, the only grandmother
I've loved, canned fourteen quarts of peaches
before gasping, stumbling, leaving us
with only her corpse and china closet.
Her sister Elsie hopes she looks this good for church,
but in such heat, she tells me, things turn.
Our backs and thighs sweat to the pews
during the sermon so full of that fiery lake
we can taste the sinners' thirst. From the grave,
families drift across the grass to older stones.
Strange, how it was a day like this in '48, they say,
in '62. It's true. August takes the mothers
in this family unexpectedly, while tomatoes burst
their skins, and sweet corn bulges with the smut
that blackens your fingers pulling back the husk.
And under this hot sun, what woman can resist—
how easy it becomes to just lie back
and let your womb swell, like all the rest.

mostly Canadians from the West—regarded plain dress as a relic of antique fashion rather than a meaningful ordinance. Many of them, migrants from Prussia and Russia in the nineteenth and early twentieth centuries, had never experienced plain dress codes. One male observer gushed in a church publication:

> Impressive was the panorama of the history of fashion—a panorama unprepared and unrehearsed yet covering at least three centuries, all the extremes and in betweens from the tieless uniformly dressed long beards to the shiny-faced, shiny-pated Florida-sport-shirted American; from the black-kerchiefed and black-shrouded ladies to the modern fuzzy-wuzzy-headed fashion doll. But between were the modestly dressed, prayer-capped ladies of the (Old) Mennonites, young and old, who in their taste and bearing, appeared almost angelic.[7]

Here is another angelic vision: not Marilyn in her white halter dress, but Mennonite women whose long hair was pinned up and crested with starched white halos, an ideal of femininity and virtue strong enough to surpass anything on the silver screen.

Gloria Steinem later wrote, "Marilyn Monroe was a female impersonator; we are all trained to be female impersonators."[8] Marilyn's impersonation of the female was part victim, part child, irresistible as a wounded bird, yet disarmingly sexual. In a nation where men had returned from war to the mass-produced satisfactions of factory work and suburban home life, this feminine exaggeration buttressed illusions of masculinity that were as damaging to men as they were to the women who felt trapped by the tasks of seduction and nurture—whatever their actual experience or knowledge may have been.

Among Mennonites, for whom the war had sorted the male sheep from the goats, there was also uncertainty about women's roles. The Mennonite female impersonator was meant to be modest and submissive, the prayer veil like a lid on any independent thoughts in her head. Of course, this image expressed neither the experience of prewar farm women—workers as strong as any Rosie the Riveter—nor of their daughters, some of whom, like my mother, were already working outside the home, even supporting their student husbands. As in broader society, the gap between the feminine ideal and women's reality was growing. How this tension played out on Sunday morning remained uncertain. Could Mennonite women lead singing? Could they teach mixed Sunday school classes? At least in the East, the postwar years saw an anxious proliferation of pamphlets and books on the topic of nonconformed dress, particularly the prayer veil—which neatly served the double function of differentiating Mennonites from the rest of society while marking their women as subordinate to men within their own group.

One sign of this anxiety is the fact that the 1963 Mennonite Confession of Faith was the first Mennonite confession of faith to identify the prayer veil as essential doctrine. This may be because the practice of wearing white caps was already endangered. *We Believe,* the 1969 interpretation of this confession, which I studied for Mennonite Church membership, features an entire chapter on the prayer veil. Obliquely referring to gender tensions in broader culture, clergyman-editor Paul Erb describes the angelic Mennonite female who keeps her head covered as a reminder of her place in a divine order: "[The head covering] urges her to remember that she is a helper, not the manager. She finds joy knowing that she willingly fits into the arrangement that God made when He created the human race, male and female. She does not want to become involved in the battle of the sexes. She wants to avoid the unhappiness of the woman who insists on having things her own way."[9]

This image reminds me of "The Angel in the House," paragon of domestic virtue and heroine of the enormously popular nineteenth-century poem written by Coventry Patmore to honor his wife. Virginia Woolf describes Patmore's Angel in her essay, "Professions for Women":

She was intensely sympathetic. She was immensely charming. She was utterly unselfish. She excelled in the difficult arts of family life. She sacrificed herself daily. If there was chicken, she took the leg; if there was a draught she sat in it—in short she was so constituted that she never had a mind or a wish of her own, but preferred to sympathize always with the minds and wishes of others. Above all—I need to say it—she was pure. Her purity was supposed to be her chief beauty—her blushes, her great grace. In those days—the last of Queen Victoria—every house had its Angel.[10]

In this passage, Woolf refers to the angel in the past tense, not because she is a thing of the past—for surely there were many such angels in attendance at the 1962 Mennonite World Conference—but because in order to publish her first book review, Woolf discovered that she could not write honestly unless she killed the Angel in her own house. And even then, she writes, "Whenever I felt the shadow of her wing or the radiance of her halo upon my page, I took up the inkpot and flung it at her."[11]

The plain-dressed, angelic Old Order and Old Mennonite women captured the imagination of Rudy Wiebe, who, in January of 1962, had become the founding editor of the *Mennonite Brethren Herald,* the Canadian Mennonite Brethren conference's first English-language publication. The cover photograph on the August 17 issue features the floor of a special women's session at the conference. Females in dress hats and shirtwaists sit on folding chairs next to others in coverings and cape dresses. In the center of the image, a young woman with a permed bob and short-sleeved gingham shift holds a child on her lap, like the Madonna. This Mennonite World Conference was the occasion of twenty-seven-year-old Rudy's first airplane ride; it was also the first time he'd seen numbers of plain-dressed Mennonites. When he returned to Winnipeg, the question of identity seemed foremost on his mind—perhaps because his own group was in the midst of its own identity crisis that expressed itself, not in questions of dress, but in a ragged and painful transition from German to English as the language for worship. Perhaps nonconformed dress served as a useful analogy for understanding cultural change at that moment: whereas prescribed language shapes the individual soul, regulation dress controls a person's body.

Women's Session, Mennonite World Conference, 1962, Kitchener, Ontario.

Rudy chose a photograph of male plain dress—a bearded, suspendered man unpacking lettuce from crates at market—for the cover of the next *Herald*. Rudy's caption: "Canadians in Ontario would immediately label this gentleman as a Mennonite; after all he is a farmer, drives a black truck, and wears black clothes and a jutting beard." Beneath the photograph, a large-type headline bluntly asks, "Who is a Mennonite?" The historically authoritative and ideologically conscious answer, excerpted from H. S. Bender's *Mennonite Encyclopedia,* is then supplied: "Mennonite: the name now given to the churches which descend from the Anabaptists from the Reformation period. . . . All groups which bear the name Mennonite, simply or with a prefix, thus claim to be in the line of historic descent . . . their legitimate claim to the title might much better be tested by their adherence to the original Anabaptist-Mennonite faith."[12]

In the previous week's issue, Rudy had printed a passage from John Howard Yoder's August 3 Mennonite World Conference address. In this sermon, Bender's brilliant young student departed from a purely historical or cultural view of identity to chastise Mennonites for their dim-witted sociological sectarianism and failures of faith:

We reason as if to live a life of love we should need to flee to some distant, less civilized place, since having more neighbors must make us less interested in their welfare. We reason as if our conscientious objection should logically cut us off from all ability to recognize in politics and history the shadings of better and worse, progress and decay. To interpret our pacifism we use the same intellectual categories—the identification of culture with dominion, of love for neighbor with hatred of the enemy, of responsibility with group egoism—from which the gospel should free us. Intellectually, this is hogwash; spiritually it is unbelief.[13]

The gist of Yoder's argument—that Mennonites must smarten up and base their identity on ideological distinction rather than tradition and social isolation—expresses the spirit of the Concern Group, to which he belonged. This circle sought to recover the essence of Anabaptism, which was more concerned with revolutionary moves of the Spirit than with the material realities of tribal identity and sacramental objects.

It may be instructive to examine a photo from John Howard Yoder's collection that captures a moment during the first meeting of the Concern Group in Amsterdam in 1952. Seven young men, dressed in dark suits and slender ties, face, not the camera and the future audiences it implies, but one another. On Easter break from their studies and voluntary relief work, they have gathered in one of the world's greatest cities: site of gruesome Anabaptist executions, yet also home of history's most culturally and intellectually engaged urban Mennonite community. A lamp glows behind David Shank's shoulder, but as in a painting from the Dutch Golden Age, light from the window illuminates everything: a page of the manuscript that Paul Peachey reads from one end of the circle, hands folded on the laps of Irvin Horst and A. Orley Swartzentruber, the leaf of a folder that John Howard Yoder has just opened, and his head bent over it. The books and polemical pamphlets haven't been published yet. These men haven't even finished their dissertations. They don't know that Orley Swartzentruber is bound to become an Episcopal priest or that Yoder,

Mennonite man at market in Kitchener, Ontario.

arguably the most influential Old Mennonite thinker of his generation, will have trouble respecting the bodies of his female students.
These farm boys and small town boys from America are so full of hope
about rebuilding Europe after the war that they believe they can create a true Anabaptist-Mennonite church that is somehow immaterial,
"in the world but not of it."

Seven years later, J. Lawrence Burkholder, a former wartime relief
pilot in India and China, wrote a Princeton dissertation that warned
against the purity and perfectionism of their ethics. Sometimes Christians have no choice but to compromise their ideals, he said, because
they have no choice but to live in a fallen world.[14] But in 1962 another,
perhaps more potent challenge to the abstract theological debates was
in production. A poster at Mennonite World Conference advertised
Rudy Wiebe's forthcoming book, *Peace Shall Destroy Many.* The theme
of this didactic first novel—that blind allegiance to Mennonite pacifism and separatism can cause schism and harbor sin—Rudy had unwittingly announced in his initial report from the conference. The
lead sentences of that article read: "Mennonites believe in fellowship.
They have often practiced separation: from the world and from each
other."[15]

The first meeting of the Concern group in Amsterdam, 1952, included (left to right) Irvin Horst, A. Orley Swartzentruber, John W. Miller, Paul Peachey, David Shank, John H. Yoder, and Calvin W. Redekop.

Two months after the conference, Rudy received his first copy of *Peace Shall Destroy Many* from Canadian publisher McClelland and Stewart. The book's title is drawn from a passage in Daniel 8 that describes the demise of a powerful, authoritarian leader:

> And in the latter time, a king shall stand up.
> And his power shall be mighty and he shall prosper.
> And he shall magnify himself in his heart, and by peace shall destroy
>   many:
> But he shall be broken without hand.[16]

In the novel, such a figure is Deacon Peter Block, who fled the violence of Soviet Russia to create a Mennonite settlement in the Canadian bush. The book opens in 1944 with protagonist Tom Wiens, pacifist plow in hand, mentally lambasting a pilot of the Royal Canadian Air Force flying above the fields of that Saskatchewan settlement. Instantly, readers see that it is impossible to form a community untouched by the outside world. As the novel unfolds, repeated reminders show that isolation does not protect a community from hypocrisy, cruelty, or violence; nor does a pacifist ideology prevent it from mistreating others. Mennonites cannot evade their own humanity, and the externalization of evil and a fearful failure to love others may be the greatest evils of all. In the final moments of the book, the protagonist learns, "Only a conquest by love unites the combatants. And in the heat of this battle lay God's peace." The novel's last line offers an ironic blessing for a fallen world: "Around the world, guns were already booming in a new day."[17]

Throughout the winter and spring following the novel's publication, Rudy continued to edit the *Mennonite Brethren Herald* amidst criticism from a constituency that felt betrayed by his unflattering representation of their group. This was Canada's first serious novel about Mennonites printed in English. Publication—by the largest book company in the country and later by Eerdmans in the United States—meant that the book would circulate broadly (an estimated 100,000 copies have been sold since 1962). That it was written in English meant that non-Mennonites could read it, and some Mennonites—including the author's own parents—could not. By June the twenty-eight-year-old father of two resigned from his post as editor of the *Herald,* under pressure from an embarrassed church board. By then, however, Wiebe had accepted an invitation to join the English department at Goshen College.

In 1964 Rudy began work on a second novel in an office he shared with sociology professor emeritus Guy F. Hershberger. Earlier in the century Hershberger, founding member of the Mennonite community movement, had nurtured H. S. Bender's sweet dreams of an isolated, tightly knit agrarian church. But in 1962 that idyllic vision of home, hearth, and fatherland had been eclipsed by other images drawn from the memory and imagination of the young novelist who shared his office.

As the story came down to me when I was a Goshen College student, probably as it is still preserved in oral tradition there, Rudy Wiebe got fired. That's what mattered. He got fired and fled into exile,

but he kept writing books, which sometimes still enrage the Mennonites. Back then, more important to me than that ideological first
novel was Wiebe's own experience. I would have to study history to
begin to understand the flap provoked by *Peace Shall Destroy Many*—
that distant war, those distant kinds of Mennonites who spoke a language I never learned. But worshiping in the church across the street
from the Mennonite Publishing House as I was growing up, I knew
exactly what it meant to publish outside the church press, and I
understood the significance of that break with ecclesiastical authority. Rudy had shown that a writer of imaginative literature—not a
church historian or sociologist or theologian—could also articulate
Mennonite identity. And this articulation—a fictitious version of
what is, rather than a factual version of what should be—was so
threatening that he got punished. I think I understood that his punishment became proof of the truth of his writing, for the Mennonite
imagination almost always makes a hero of a fugitive-martyr.

In many ways, however, I now see that Wiebe could not be my
model, even as he was and continues to be an important figure in my
life. Because I was born female in the early 1960s, my relationship to
culture and the church was quite different from Wiebe's and that of
his generation. During the 1970s, I wore a "Menno Power" T-shirt to
a consolidated public high school, although none of my classmates
realized that the beanie-topped, wrinkled face on my chest belonged
to Menno Simons, the great Dutch Mennonite preacher and writer.
My uncle, who had marched in civil rights protests with students from
Eastern Mennonite College (now University) and done relief work in
Vietnam with Mennonite Central Committee during the war, was my
countercultural hero. When I got baptized in 1976, I could choose
whether to wear a prayer veil or not. And I continued wearing it to
church even after my mother, who never had such a choice, quit wearing hers, because I valued that symbol of Anabaptist-Mennonite identity. Following the politics of a radical Jesus, I just assumed I could
ignore the old ideas about female submission. Although a few of my
early poems were published in *With,* the mod Mennonite youth mag-

azine, I was not being groomed to become a prince of the church. Given the evidence at hand, I would have worked only with children's literature if I had become an editor at the Mennonite Publishing House. I never dreamed of writing a book that could contend with Bender's or of gaining the European university credentials favored by Mennonite leaders of his and later generations. Great freedom came with slight expectations.

My turn to imaginative writing, unlike Rudy's, was not a betrayal of my potential to become a church leader. For poetry seemed to belong in some other, "worldly" compartment of my life, separate and safe from censure or community judgment. My earliest poems may have sounded like hymns, but I learned to write free verse in public school, once exactly replicating the syntax of the teacher's model—until I realized that each free verse poem could find its own form. In college I fell in love with the red wheelbarrow and white chickens of William Carlos Williams. His imagist slogan, "Not in ideas, but in things," suited my Anabaptist sensibility, which, if it had been articulate at all, would have resounded in agreement, "Not in creeds, but in deeds." In my early twenties I adopted as my exemplar H. D., the modernist poet about whom I wrote an undergraduate thesis at New York University. (Did all the powerful authors only go by their initials back then?)

H. D. (Hilda Doolittle) grew up in a Pennsylvania Moravian family but followed Ezra Pound to London early in the twentieth century. A theatrical beauty and passionate lover of several great modernist authors, she found that the female writer must finally become a kind of hermaphrodite, her own muse, if she is to shift from being the subject of men's poems to becoming the author of her own writing and her own life. This is the shift that Marilyn Monroe never managed to make, although she sought serious acting roles later in her career. Robert Bly, gender-conscious bard who in the past thirty years has celebrated both the Great Mother and Iron John, believes that Marilyn's remarkable appeal and her suicide were the consequence of this failure. Her persona invited viewers of both sexes to project onto her an extreme feminine image during those highly gendered postwar years. "Thousands, even millions of American men projected their internal feminine onto Marilyn Monroe," Bly writes. "If a million men do that, and leave it there, it's likely she will die. She died."[18] (As I write this, it alarms me that this essay is filling up with so many dead bodies, but perhaps they are warnings that it takes a death to make an angel—a woman giving up self-interest can lose her own life.)

H. D. refused to give up her expatriate life even during the war years, and she produced a substantial body of literary work before her death in 1961. I think I understand why she remained abroad, writing her great epics through veils of mythical allusion. American female poets who followed her have managed—sometimes at the cost of their own lives—to overcome those kinds of evasions and to write more directly from their experience as bodies in the world.[19] Their hard-won advances have been my encouragement, and I feel fortunate to follow them. Those poets and many others since them have begun to do what Virginia Woolf could not do, and what ultimately must have contributed to her suicide. In her lecture to the Woman's Service League, she admits her triumph and her failure as a writer: "These were two of the adventures of my professional life. The first—killing the Angel in the House—I think I solved. She died. But the second, telling the truth about my own experiences as a body, I do not think I solved. I doubt that any woman has solved it yet."[20] This was a truth difficult to tell because so few could bear to hear it.

Changes in American culture and in the Mennonite community have brought the book and the female body into closer proximity, nor is Bender now as far from Marilyn as he was in 1962. This book is partial proof of that. The brochure that advertised the academic conference for which this essay was initially written depicted as featured speakers two individuals—Stanley Hauerwas and myself. The larger of the two speakers' photographs is a conventional head-and-shoulders shot of a bald Duke University professor who has established a distinguished reputation by writing and publishing many books about ethics. The smaller photograph is the shot of the author from *Eve's Striptease,* a collection of poems that tries to make sense of female experience and the female body. "Outwardly, what is simpler than to write books? Outwardly, what obstacles are there for a woman rather than for a man? Inwardly, I think, the case is very different; she has still many ghosts to fight, many prejudices to overcome," wrote Woolf just before World War II.[21] Does my photograph, taken in front of a fan like a fashion shot and typical of a certain group of women writers that some have called "the hair poets," suggest that a warm gust from Marilyn's subway has blown across my face?

A while ago, as I was having coffee with Lancaster County writer Louise Stoltzfus, I described my frustrating struggle to discover what significance lay in the story about H. S. Bender and Marilyn Monroe. I told her that I knew there was something important beyond the details of that story, but I just couldn't get at it. Louise thought a moment and then said, "Hey! I wonder whether Marilyn's death hit people the way the death of Princess Di did."

Instantly, I knew she must be right: two blond women in their thirties undone by too much attention. Consorts of prince and president, victims of the press and also of a desire for celebrity within themselves, something about them seemed so fawn-like and innocent and pure—despite all that we know about their lives; something about their irresistible, sad eyes, their gorgeous white dresses, and their beautiful bodies within them.

I first heard the news of Diana's death kneeling in Saint Stephen's Cathedral Church on Front Street in Harrisburg, Pennsylvania, as someone prayed for the repose of the soul of Lady Diana of York and the others who were killed in the car with her. At that moment I was suddenly struck self-conscious: a Mennonite praying for a dead person is odd enough, but praying for a divorced member of the British Royal family? At last, I thought in a fit of hyperbole, I have sold my birthright for a bowl of pottage—weekly Eucharist and liturgical language. I have jumped the fence, "thrown off the traces," sold the farm, nearly five hundred years of cultural resistance down the drain, which might as well be the river where they drowned Anabaptist martyr Felix Manz. I am "the Englisch." This was no light riff for a daughter of Bender, no matter how distant. But what Louise told me next was a kind of sweet assurance, proof that the ideal of cultural purity has always been an impossible fiction.

That same Sunday morning at Blossom Hill, her Mennonite church in Lancaster County, the preacher had shocked the congregation by saying that, even though he couldn't quite approve of Lady Diana's lifestyle, her death was a great tragedy. Louise found herself oddly shaken for the rest of the day. Assuming that her Amish parents had not yet heard the news, she called them that afternoon. Oh yes, they said, they'd heard about it in church that morning. The preacher had mentioned it.

And how had the preacher known of Diana's death without owning a radio, let alone a TV?

"Well," Louise told me, "the preacher's wife listens to a police scanner—for some reason that's permitted by the church—and maybe the news of Diana's death had come over that."

CAMP HILL, 1998

The Gothic Tale of Lucy Hochstetler
and the Temptation of Literary Authority

9 One cold Sunday evening in the winter of 1948, a Conservative Conference Mennonite woman and her husband were invited to dine with the seventy-five-year-old widowed Amish Bishop Samuel Hochstetler in his home about seven miles east of Goshen, Indiana. During supper, the guests heard sounds that seemed to be human moans and the muffled rattling of chains. When questioned, the bishop explained that these noises were nothing to be concerned about; one often heard such sounds on a farm. The female guest was so troubled, however, that she could not sleep that night, and the next day she sent her father to speak with Goshen's deputy sheriff, former Amishman Levi Bontrager.[1]

From a legal perspective, the case was mismanaged at the outset. After questioning some neighbors who offered little help, Deputy Bontrager and Sheriff Luther Yoder visited the Hochstetler home without a search warrant on the afternoon of January 21. When they arrived, the bishop was out in the barn, and his nineteen-year-old granddaughter, Miriam, answered the door. While Miriam was calling her grandfather in from the straw shed, the sheriff and his deputy pushed open a door on the first floor of the farmhouse and discovered forty-one-year-old Lucy Hochstetler, unkempt and apparently deranged, chained to her bed in a dirty, dark, unventilated room. After a brief conversation with the white-bearded bishop, the officers left, only to return the next day with newspaper reporters, photographers, and a warrant for the bishop's arrest on charges of assault and battery. They took the old man to the Elkhart County Circuit Court, where he was arraigned and jailed. More photographs were taken. Early the next morning, before his children, who were traveling by horse-drawn buggy, had time to arrive, Bishop Hochstetler was tried without legal counsel. He pleaded guilty and was sentenced to six months labor on the state penal farm.

A transcript of the trial suggests that Hochstetler was probably confused by the judge's line of questioning, although he tried to explain that it had become necessary to chain Lucy to her bed because she was sometimes dangerous to herself and to others, and she was stronger than his wife, who had died that November. The judge scolded the bishop, portraying him as an ignorant primitive: "I am sending you down to the State Farm for six months as punishment for doing this inhuman act. A man of your age and intelligence should know better, in a civilized world." The judge also ordered that Lucy be examined by physicians, who found her to be insane but healthy, showing no signs of physical abuse. She was then removed from her community and placed in a state mental institution.[2]

A 1997 article by Japanese scholar Mami Hiraike Okawara posits that a teenage romance may have been the source, or at least a contributing factor, in Lucy's mental illness. Okawara uncovered evidence that Lucy—said to have been a bright and popular student in public school—had fallen in love with a non-Amish classmate a year *after* she had joined the Amish church at the age of fifteen. Because she was a church member, marriage to an outsider would have necessitated shunning and expulsion from the community, so her parents were opposed to the relationship. They forbade her to date the boy, and her mother beat her when she discovered that he had given Lucy a scarf and box of candy. Lucy then ran away from home and secured a position as a domestic worker in Goshen.

Up to this point, Lucy's story is an uncanny echo of the plots of several early- or mid-twentieth-century local color romances that depict an intelligent Amish or Mennonite maiden who manages to rise above her oppressive background through a romance with a charming outsider. These books—like *Tillie, a Mennonite Maid; Sabina, a Story of the Amish;* or *Maggie of Virginsburg*—were written by women like Helen R. Martin, who lived near Amish or Mennonite communities but who did not belong to them. Accordingly, the novels depict accurate and authenticating details of plain, rural life, even as they are populated by a cast of grossly stereotypical characters. The fathers are portrayed as tyrannical taskmasters, greedy for land and money, who forbid their children to read or participate in public education and who practice a severe and punishing religion that is especially cruel to their work-worn, submissive wives. Whereas romance is the most obvious force in the daughter's liberation, public education and progressive Christian ideals are often additional factors. The girl invariably leaves home to become a schoolteacher, the wife of her dashing nonsectarian suitor, or some other happy-ever-after fulfillment of a plain girl's destiny.

This pattern of escape through romance and education is common in local color novels written during this period that represent other minority groups as well. These books support the American ideal of assimilation into the democratic melting pot, often by way of public school. Furthermore, they seem to be influenced both by the progressive ideal of female emancipation and by a simultaneous anxiety about female emancipation, so that the young women escape the controlling grasp of their Amish fathers only by running into the arms of non-Amish American lovers. One such novel was the highly popular *Straw in the Wind,* published in 1937, approximately a decade before Lucy's case came to trial. Set in Middlebury, Indiana, a town near Lucy's home, the book was written by a local author, Ruth Lininger Dobson. It won the prestigious Hopwood prize from the University of

Michigan and received substantial local press upon its publication—
including negative responses from local Amish spokesmen who felt
that the book misrepresented their group.

The novel follows the demise of an abusive Amish patriarch, Moses
Bontrager. During the course of the story, the man's wife dies from
overwork and consumption; one daughter—while employed as a domestic worker in town—is seen listening to dance music and therefore
is shunned before she runs away from home and finds a worldly boy-
friend; and another daughter manages to sustain a secret courtship
with an Amish-Mennonite beau. It is likely that some who observed
the Lucy case in northern Indiana would have read or recalled the
publicity that surrounded *Straw in the Wind,* and it may be that the
novel influenced some perceptions of Lucy's case. But the parallel between Lucy Hochstetler's romance and the happy-ever-after scenar-
ios of Rebecca and Polly Bontrager ceases when Lucy's story takes an
abrupt and disturbingly gothic departure from the conventional ro-
mantic plot.

After a month of living as a domestic worker in a Goshen household, Lucy was discovered by her parents and forced to return to the
family farm. According to Okawara's account, Lucy's parents sometimes tied her to trees with a rope when she was working outdoors to
keep her from running away again. Okawara believes it was after Lucy
was forced to return to the farm that she developed symptoms of depression and seizures diagnosed as St. Vitas' Dance, or chorea. Her illness led her parents to seek medical treatment in Goshen and eventually in Chicago. None of the treatments—perhaps including some
kind of surgery—seemed to remedy Lucy's condition; in fact, it wors-
ened. After Lucy repeatedly chewed through her rope restraints, they
were replaced with chains attached to bull rings worn on her wrists, as
verified by several sources. Nevertheless, a state health worker who
visited the family in 1944 concluded that Lucy was probably better off
at home than she would have been in a public mental health institution of that day.

After being placed in the care of the state in 1948, Lucy improved only slightly. Twenty-four years later, she was transferred to the custody of her nephew, who in 1972 moved her to the Goshen Nursing Home, where she died in 1978 at the age of seventy-one. My research uncovered no letters, school papers, or other firsthand representations of Lucy's language or experience. In a court record of the case, a brief but revealing exchange between the Pennsylvania German (Dutch)–speaking sheriff and the bishop suggests that Lucy did not speak to the lawmen about her confinement and only uttered a word after her father responded to a question directed at her:

Sheriff: She wouldn't talk to us out there. She would whine a little or murmur a little, but it wasn't intelligible and you really didn't know whether she was crying or just whining.

Bishop: She answered you, didn't she? You asked her if she was—

Sheriff: That is right. I asked her in Dutch if that hurt her wrists and *you* answered that it wouldn't, and then she said no in Dutch [emphasis mine].

Who are the voiceless bodies in this story? They are Lucy, of course, and her father, who faced trial without the assistance of an attorney. In the course of events, the bishop also came to represent the Amish community that was misunderstood and persecuted by the dominating American society during World War II, so the religious community becomes a third silent body.

Who are the authors? There is the judge, who names the bishop's behavior "uncivilized" and narrates his punishment, and there are

"Samuel Hochstetler, 75-year-old Amish bishop, clutched a Bible in one hand as he submitted the other for fingerprinting in the Elkhart county jail in Goshen, Ind., today. He was sentenced to 6 months in a state penal farm on charges of assault and battery after officers discovered his 41-year-old daughter chained to her bed Thursday. Taking fingerprints is chief deputy Sheriff Levi Bontrager."

the journalists. Captioned pictures of Lucy and her father—taken in violation of Amish beliefs that forbid photography—were syndicated in newspapers across the United States and as far away as South America and Europe. In this country, the story may have satisfied a lingering animosity that some Americans felt toward members of the peace churches and their German-speaking patriarchs, embodied in the photograph of a stern-faced, white-bearded bishop in plain dress holding a Bible in one hand as the deputy sheriff takes fingerprints from his other hand. The capture and punishment of the bishop may have presented a subtle analogue of America's defeat of the uniformed, anti-democratic tyrants in Europe. The longing for self-determination to triumph over compliance and tradition was running deep in the postwar American spirit, and some newspaper accounts claimed that Lucy had been confined to her bed because she wished to leave the Amish church. (In another report, it must be noted, Lucy's brother, Elam, explained that this was untrue, that Lucy had joined the Amish church at the age of fifteen, and that she was later restrained only because she had become violent and disoriented.) Beyond American borders, the story fueled anti-Protestant sentiment in Catholic countries in Europe and South America. A headline in Italy read: "Protestant Bishop Chains Daughter to Bed."[3]

I cannot ignore the authority or interests of the external voices who

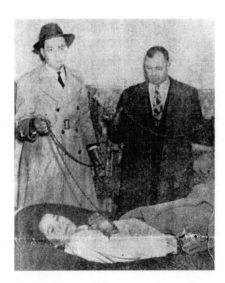

"Sheriff Luther Yoder, right, and Chief Deputy Levi Bontrager, of Elkhart county, hold the chains which bound Lucy Hochstettler [sic] to her bed in her father's home near Goshen, Ind. This picture was made before the woman was released."

authored Lucy's story, including even the Japanese scholar who thoroughly pursued the case. My email exchanges with Okawara have been appropriately gracious and impersonal, yet I cannot help but wonder if the figure of Lucy, a victim of constraint in a formal and traditional society, does not elicit special sympathy from a woman on the faculty of a Japanese city university of economics. I wonder whether this Asian scholar of American Studies does not find in her work some of the cultural parallels I felt as an American student studying in China and later minoring in East Asian studies at New York University. For instance, does she see that the Japanese tendency to feel shame—experienced as transgression of the group's expectations—is more akin to Amish cultural ways than the typical Westerner's individually internalized feeling of guilt for a misdeed?[4] Do the Japanese concepts of *amae* (an individual's reliance on others or the collective system) and *tatemae* and *honne* (the official view that often must supersede an individual's actual opinion) seem similar to the Amish value of mutual aid and the social control of *Gelassenheit,* an individual's spirit of yieldedness to the norms of Anabaptist society? Does she also see a parallel emphasis on honoring elders and respecting tradition in both cultures—as well as a parallel threat to those old values, beginning after World War II but continuing into the present?

As fascinating as these speculations may seem, I fear that they paint both cultures too broadly, and I prefer to examine the particular and to focus on the ways that Amish and Mennonite authors responded to the representations of their community. Among these writers are Miriam Hochstetler, Lucy's niece; Guy F. Hershberger and John Umble, Goshen College professors who became involved in the case; ex-Amish writer J. W. Yoder; Mennonite churchman J. C. Wenger; and, finally, myself.[5]

Miriam Hochstetler, the bishop's granddaughter, became an author in this story by accident and out of necessity, probably at the urging of others. Her text responds to the community's most urgent needs. She is the person who first spotted two strangers coming in the lane of the Hochstetler farm on that January afternoon. Four days later, she carefully wrote a six-page account of events under the familiar biblical epigraph, "All things work together for good to them that love the Lord." Her text, handwritten on loose-leaf paper, was deposited and preserved in the Samuel D. Hochstetler files in the Mennonite Archives at Goshen College, among other articles and papers pertaining to the case. Miriam's authority comes from experience: she was an eyewitness, and her report is mostly motivated by outrage at the inaccuracy of the newspaper reports. To tell a lie is sin enough, but to willfully publish untruths is scandalous to people who belong to a culture that understands the primary function of writing and print text to be the preservation of factual records or spiritual truths.[6] Initially, Miriam admits that Lucy was in bad shape when the civil authorities first found her, but she resents the exaggerated reports that claimed Lucy was bruised and bloody from the chains: "Oh, they thought it was awful. It was. She hadn't been combed for quite a while. Her room was in a mess and a half. Her clothes weren't too clean either, but they wouldn't have to put a lot of untruths in the paper."

Her text continues to describe the sheriff's second visit and sincerely expresses her terror and sense of helplessness at the intrusion of the lawmen and reporters. She regards the strangers as aliens, using collective pronouns to refer to "one of them" and "the other." And although deeply shaken, Miriam cannot resist poking fun at a reporter's unlit cigar:

> Shivers went from head to toes. There was nothing else to do so I opened the door. Four officers, the two sheriffs and two dumb looking fellows asked to see "Sam." One of them had on a "hard looking" cap & large dark rimmed glasses. The other carried something with his mouth. Hard work I'd think to keep such a heavy thing balanced. But seems some people get a lot of joy out of it. Didn't see any smoke come from it so he probably had it there for the looks.

Given no choice but to open the door to the men who came to arrest her grandfather and photograph Lucy, Miriam describes feelings of defenselessness and violation, while expressing the Amish sense of separation between their own homes and community and the external world, even hinting at a sense of moral superiority to that world. Her ability to find humor at the expense of the trench-coated, "dumb looking" men undermines, in a small way, the power that the state and media exercised over her family by removing Lucy from her home, publishing the photographs, and calling the bishop a demeaning nickname in his own house.

Miriam concludes her account by voicing the shock and confusion shared by her community and family. Apart from humor and prayer, there seems to be little defense against the powerful forces and opinion of the dominating culture. Miriam's parents were the only Amish people in a crowd of approximately fifty Goshen citizens who gathered for the bishop's trial that morning, and newspaper publicity further isolated and exposed the Amish community to the scrutiny and judgment of the American mainstream. Significantly, by the end of her text, Miriam writes as "we," rather than "I," hoping to comfort and encourage herself and her readers as they contemplate the bishop's sentence: "We think there's got to be done something soon for the poor man that he doesn't have to stay his six months. If God doesn't want him to be there that long he'll make a way."

A way for the bishop's release was made through the efforts of John Umble and Guy F. Hershberger, two Goshen College professors who rallied the support of the Mennonite community and assisted the bishop's family in petitioning the governor of Indiana. Umble and Hershberger saw in the Hochstetler case a familiar story: the dominant culture had failed to understand and respect Amish ways and therefore had wrongly persecuted an innocent man. With fresh memories of wartime hostility toward pacifist groups, they saw in the judge's decision an anti-Amish/anti-Mennonite gesture, and they rushed to rescue the bishop from this miscarriage of justice and public disgrace. As members of the educated elite of their generation and of H. S. Bender's circle of Mennonite scholars at Goshen, these men no doubt believed that their God-given abilities and their educational advantages bound them to use their gifts in the service and interests of the community—even to engage in political advocacy.

A few days after Hochstetler's trial, John Umble, an English and speech professor who grew up in an Amish home, wrote a letter to the *Goshen News-Democrat* to condemn the unwarranted and rapid arrest of the Amish bishop, charging that the court did not understand or respect Amish life. In February, Umble published a longer article in *Gospel Herald,* the national Mennonite weekly magazine, titled "Justice Fails Again," in which he reported information gathered from the Hochstetler family to set the public record straight. The legal system misunderstood rural life and Amish ways of caring for the disabled, he explained, and it misjudged a respectable father and church leader. Umble urged Mennonite brothers and sisters in faith to support the persecuted bishop, following the biblical injunction and Anabaptist ideal to "bear one another's burdens." The article was reprinted in the *Daily Intelligencer Journal* in Lancaster, Pennsylvania, with an introductory note explaining that "relatives and friends and members of the peace churches are particularly aroused" over false newspaper reports that Lucy was chained because she refused to remain part of her religious group. Umble's article was among materials appended to the petition submitted to the governor of Indiana, who, at the recommendation of a clemency board, granted an early parole—but not a pardon—before the bishop had served half his sentence.[7]

To obtain the parole, Guy F. Hershberger helped Hochstetler family members write letters to local newspapers, and Hershberger drafted the request for the bishop's pardon on grounds that Hochstetler was "an honorable and substantial citizen" and that Lucy was "well cared for." Knowing of the inhumane conditions in state mental institutions from reports of Mennonite men who had worked in them during their terms of Civilian Public Service, Hershberger tried to establish that Lucy would have received far worse treatment under the care of the state. These actions seem to be consistent with the career of the Goshen College sociologist, who was a founding member of the Mennonite Community Association, which advocated the preservation of religious village life. The Mennonite community movement emerged in response to urbanization, cultural assimilation, and the distressing fact that in spite of the denomination's pacifist beliefs, more than half of all Mennonites who were drafted served in some capacity during World War II.[8] Hershberger's involvement in the Lucy case prefigured his later efforts to speak on behalf of Iowa Amish in their disputes with the state over mandatory public high school attendance policies. At the heart of his actions is the paradoxical demand that a democratic society respect the right of a group to exercise nondemocratic constraints on its own members, as in the case of Lucy, and to abstain from involvement in those public institutions, such as public schooling, which exist largely to sustain the democratic system.

Umble and Hershberger spoke immediately and effectively on behalf of the inarticulate Amish bishop, but they seem to have remained silent concerning his voiceless daughter. This must be because they believed that she was better off in her family's care than she would have been in a public institution. Moreover, I believe that the aged, defenseless bishop represented for them the ever-endangered traditional community. Both Hershberger and Umble were among mid-twentieth-century intellectually elite Mennonites who viewed rural Amish and Mennonite communities with an attitude of protectionism and preservationism—and who gained authority by speaking on behalf of these groups. Hershberger studied and defended Mennonite community life as a sociological phenomenon, and Umble found in his heritage subjects for folk and cultural study. Both men gained entrance into scholarly communities, as I have, by writing about the folk cultures of their own backgrounds. Moreover, during the war years, when American masculinity was established by a soldier's ability to protect his wife and children at home through combat abroad, Mennonite leaders, authoritarian males for the most part, negotiated with government officials in Washington, D.C., to protect the beliefs of a vulnerable and voiceless community back home. Vivid in the memory of Amish and Mennonite people was the mistreatment of pacifists in army boot camps during World War I and the death of a young Amishman during incarceration in a Kansas penitentiary during World War II. On behalf of the silent bishop and the community he signified, the Goshen professors were thus bound to confront the media and even the governor, overlooking Lucy's circumstances.

On the other hand, their contemporary, Amish-Mennonite J. W. Yoder, immediately identified with Lucy. In the story "Amish Bishop Keeps Daughter Chained to Filthy Bed 10 Years," printed on January 23 in his local Huntingdon, Pennsylvania, newspaper, Yoder saw, not the persecution of a defenseless leader of a peace church, but *bondage*—physical and spiritual—a brutality inflicted on a woman by her father and bishop. On seeing the report, Yoder suspected that the source of Lucy's illness could be traced to the constraints of Amish culture, and he urged state intervention. He hastily dashed a letter off to Sheriff Luther Yoder, whom he addressed as "My dear Kinsman" (although they appear to be unrelated): "The definite point that I want to know is whether Hochstetler in any way punished his daughter to compel her to stay in his church before she lost her mind. That is THE point. And of course, that is what the Law wants to know."[9] Yoder, by then in his seventies, explained to the sheriff that he had grown up in a Pennsylvania Amish home and had not joined his parents' church, thus situating himself in relation to Lucy's situation.

While Yoder may have been reacting in response to his own ambivalent feelings about his Amish preacher father and strict bishop grandfather, he also recognized and admitted that his personal position informed his perception of Lucy's situation. This strategy is similar to the ways that he used his own experience and desire for education and wider experience to imagine and portray his mother's life in *Rosanna of the Amish,* a nostalgic work of biography and memoir. In fact, voiceless bodies and personal analogy continued to sustain Yoder's literary authority: after writing his mother's story, he became an advocate for a man who had been shunned by an Old Order group during the mid-1940s. In 1950, partly as a consequence of that shunning, he published a bombastic, book-length challenge to Amish religious practices. And four years later, his final work focused solely on the doctrine of the prayer veil, or head covering, which he called "the veil of subordination." Speaking on behalf of the mass of silent, plain-dressed Mennonite and Amish women, he sought to reform Amish and Mennonite patriarchy through reason and scholarly theological argument.

In Yoder, I see the beginning of a literary authority that draws its power from the specific, particular, and therefore deeply humble "I" of individual perception in conversation with, and expressive of, imaginative empathy for others. But the transition from the "we"-minded political or ecclesiastical authority of Umble and Hershberger to the empathic "I" of authentic writerly authority and dialogue was not smooth—nor is it complete, as the next appropriation of the Lucy story demonstrates.

In September of 1980, theologian and church historian J. C. Wenger published an interpretation of the Lucy Hochstetler story in the weekly national newspaper *The Mennonite Reporter.* In a two-article sequence of his column, "Anecdotes from Mennonite History," Wenger offers a most bizarre example of Mennonite historical imagination and genealogical obsession, noting that the defenseless bishop Samuel Hochstetler was a descendant—through both his mother's and father's lines—of the immigrant Jacob Hochstetler. This well-known ancestor refused to bear arms in a 1757 Delaware Indian raid and was therefore taken into captivity with three of his sons. Jacob Hochstetler's wife and another child were killed in the attack on their Berks County, Pennsylvania, homestead.

Following this ancestor, Bishop Hochstetler is portrayed as a meek believer who remained faithful in the face of persecution, forgiving his accusers and feeling no bitterness for his sentence. Of his stay at the penal farm, the bishop is quoted as having written, "The boss sometimes called me 'Dad,' and also asked me to return thanks at meals. I had a nice room, good warm bed, a rocking chair and stand where I could read my good Bible, also a little dark room to go in and pray." Wenger praises the Goshen professors who fostered a spirit of mutual aid among many in the Anabaptist community and who assisted in the bishop's release, and he calls Hochstetler a "true son of the non-resistant Jacob." With the memory of sixteenth-century martyrs and the colonial progenitor in view, Lucy's more immediate plight is easily pushed out of sight. Like all writers of history, Wenger gains authority by speaking for the dead—yet another category of a voiceless body. A seminary professor and the youngest and perhaps most loyal member of the mid-twentieth-century H. S. Bender circle, Wenger carried the banner of Mennonite identity and tradition into the latter half of the century, authoring *Separated Unto God,* a thoughtful justification of nonconformity and nonresistance, and wearing his plain coat into the 1980s. Like the Goshen professors, Wenger saw in Lucy's story the pattern of a larger story about Anabaptist nonresistance and persecution at the hands of the secular state.

I too am a writer who gains authority by telling this story. Lucy first captured my imagination when I came across newspaper clippings and letters in the archive at Juniata College during the summer of 1995 when I was gathering information for my dissertation on J. W. Yoder. I must have recognized in the photographs of a young woman, bound and close-mouthed, a figure for all the silent and confined women I have known—silent only in public, of course, and confined only to the eternal tasks of housework and domestic duty. How strange that Lucy's story hit the press the same year that my Amish grandmother—three years younger than Lucy and a mother of five—died in a buggy accident. Although this episode was a minor note in the life of the man I was studying, I was haunted by a vision of Lucy gnawing those ropes, trying to free herself with her mouth—as I try to free myself with my mouth, roughly, crudely attempting to articulate whatever I am able to say. "You have such a sharp tongue, it's a wonder you have any friends at all," I heard growing up. But through the years that "tongue" has become blunted. When I was about to publish *Sleeping Preacher,* I feared that I had written myself out of my home community altogether, but if anything, those poems have bound me to the community more tightly than before, marking me as a "Mennonite writer."

Now I see that the Lucy story offers me two conventional visions of female literary authority. In Miriam, the dutiful bishop's niece, I see a young woman who was able to write for all of history the official version of the community's victimization at the hands of civil authorities. She is the scribe who writes as "we" in the best interests of the group. In Lucy, I see a madwoman, or *The Madwoman in the Attic*—to borrow the title of a brilliant historical study of female literary authority. In this book, Sandra Gilbert and Susan Gubar explain that women writing during the nineteenth century found themselves trapped in their father's (or husband's) houses and circumscribed within the texts of the male literary tradition that describe both the world and women's place in it. Absence of female precursors created a "veiled vision" for these writers who lacked access to their own literary authority. The Gothic novels of this era are full of girls and women confined to stuffy rooms and narrow roles, fettered, imprisoned, chained in the attic, or buried alive. Gilbert and Gubar argue that these figures express for the anxious female author the danger of repressed anger and the fearful consequences of her desire for rebellious escape from male-dominated houses and male-shaped stories.[10]

With these ideas in mind, Lucy is my mad double—both furious and insane—whom I fear I will become in the eyes of others if I write in defiance of social expectations or traditional precedents. She is especially in view these days as I work at Messiah College with students who subscribe to various forms of conservative Christianity, the domain of patriarchal religious norms and language scripted to ensure belonging within specific holy houses. Here I keenly feel the expectations I write to resist, although they are often only internalized as shame or as a vague sense of transgression. Will I be Miriam, the dutiful scribe, or Lucy, raging in my chains?

In a remarkable passage of the trial's transcript, the bishop portrays Lucy as a mute madwoman whose illness was manifested in her attempts at escape, in violence against her caregiver mother, and, most significant to this metaphoric meaning, in the destruction of books:

Bishop: She was stout and she ran away sometimes.

Court: Ran away?

Bishop: Yes. Before that, not so much then any more, but upstairs and took books and tore them up sometimes and wasn't safe, and she wasn't hardly safe to have her loose by herself.

Court: Did she ever threaten you in any way?

Bishop: Not me, but my wife.

Court: She threatened your wife.

Bishop: Yes.

Court: What did she say?

Bishop: Oh, didn't say much, she was pretty rough with her. At just times. Not all of the time.

Court: Did she give any reason for being rough or—

Bishop: No. Her mind was failing. That was the trouble.

Elsewhere in the trial, this image of the violent monster who "didn't say much" is contrasted with a cherubic singer who doesn't say much either. When asked about Lucy's attitude toward the Amish church as she got older, her father replied, "Well, she don't say much, but she sings spiritual songs that I didn't know she knowed. Hours and hours she sang songs, but when she was by herself. But if she was out with us and other people there she wouldn't talk much." Lucy was either a deranged monster or an angel, but always not quite human, trapped outside the conversations of normal community discourse.

We know that Lucy did attempt to escape this community in her youth, perhaps driven by her own desires, but she was captured and returned to her father's house, fettered first with ropes, then with chains. A story that circulated in the community after she was discovered by the authorities claimed that Lucy could feel her "fits" coming on and actually asked to be manacled at those times.[11] Whether or not this is true, it certainly supports the metaphor of the madwoman who fears the destructive force of her own repressed rage and claustrophobia, and who attempts to control her anger because she knows that the consequence of expressing such powerful feelings are only isolation and punishment. When Lucy was delivered from her father's house into the hands of the state, she was confined once again, this time in a place where conditions may have been far more alienating than those back at her father's farm, and she remains a figure trapped in mostly male-authored texts.

Lucy is a figure in the text that I am writing also. She is the silent subject who becomes a metaphor for the madwoman I sometimes feel myself to be as I write texts to realize my own anger, texts that cause me to worry about whether others will consider me to be mistaken or even crazy. Moreover, Lucy reminds me of all the silent people whose stories I have told in order to become an author. I am thinking, for instance, of my parents, who left an Amish-Mennonite farm valley in the 1950s and who worked hard and quietly to make a home for us in the wider world. Or I am thinking of my plain and non-plain relatives who stayed there. I became an author by writing the stories of these people.

Only after a book was published did my guilt and curiosity cause me to engage the subjects of those poems in conversations about how it felt to be represented, and I found those conversations almost too painful to bear. In one letter, an older woman responded to my questions about how my book was being received by some relatives in the Valley:

> I understand what upset [another great-aunt]. I think it would have hurt me too if a relative of mine had drug all that stuff into a book even if I know it happened. I'm not saying these things aren't true but I am trying to point out to you that it was a bad enough hurt to have happened, and then drag it into a book. I understand but it is your family too. I don't like to say that but I was to be truthful. Doesn't poetry need to rhyme any more? It used to be that way but I suppose it changed. Are you expressing some mixed up feelings you have about the Mennonite faith????

In my poems, she sees not quite madness, but some "mixed up feelings" expressed in the betrayals of family loyalty, poetic tradition, and religious belief. Her own commitment to truth telling compels her to

A FAMILY HISTORY

At dusk the girl who will become my mom
must trudge through the snow, her legs
cold under skirts, a bandanna tight on her braids.
In the henhouse, a klook pecks her chapped hand
as she pulls a warm egg from under its breast.
This girl will always hate hens,
and she already knows she won't marry a farmer.
In a dim barn, my father, a boy, forks hay
under the Holsteins' steaming noses.
They sway on their hooves and swat dangerous tails,
but he is thinking of snow, how it blows
across the gray pond scribbled with skate tracks,
of the small blaze on its shore, and the boys
in black coats who shake hand-in-hand
round and round, building up speed
until the leader cracks that whip
of mittens and arms, and it jerks around
fast, flinging off the last boy.
He'd be that one—flung like a spark
trailing only his scarf.

tell me this. Of these betrayals, only the transgression of literary convention can be forgiven because "it changed"; the others are simply disturbing and baffling, so much as to require excessive punctuation. Likely, "the hurt" is not just lodged in the past or with the other silent relative on whose behalf she speaks.

I replied to this letter by explaining my belief in the importance of "talk" about even difficult things in communities and families, and my desire to make sense of my heritage. In her reply, she imagined what might cause me to "drag all that stuff into a book," although my good memory and ability to do "a good job of it"—present things in a realistic way—still seem no excuse for exposing the community's sensitive secrets:

> Now I can just see you writing down what you remember of your childhood, what you heard your mother and aunts talk about their father in hushed tones—but Julia heard [and] now she is putting that into a book. That changes the whole picture. To be honest very few people know all those things as we here in the Valley do so you see it was hard for me to hurt you when you do a good job of it. [12]

Wise as any literary theorist, she knows that writing and publishing change "the whole picture"—for both the object and the subject of the text.

Lucy's story reminds me of how tempting it is for authors to give up writing from the humble and specific and difficult position of "I" and take on the more general and broadly sanctioned "we." In an essay about political poetry, Irish poet Evan Boland speaks of the "subtle claim" of the political poem, the poem that speaks for "we." In such poems, as in the Lucy stories, the voice of the subject becomes "all-powerful," and the object "would not just be silent. It would be silenced." [13] Compelled by public interest, this kind of poem reduces the complexity of the community, it is easy to write and easy to publish, and it swiftly establishes the authority of its writer.

The temptation of writing as "we" has never been greater for Mennonite and other minority or ethnic American authors. These days a Mennonite author can gain approval and recognition from both secular academics and Mennonite church leaders. Multicultural enthusiasts and scholars are eager to endorse texts that represent American minorities, and they unwittingly create exotic ghettos for them in the literary canon, even though authenticity finally comes, not from ethnic signatures, but from the complexity of situated individual perceptions. As for church authorities, I can only guess what purpose is served by embracing Mennonite literature: certainly it promotes ethnic identity and bolsters group pride, and it demonstrates a new openness to the arts, so unlike the repressive old days. But as some leaders now stand by or enforce new forms of shunning and silence in the community, they overlook gay and lesbian bodies just as the Goshen professors overlooked Lucy years ago.

The totalizing "we" that constructs group identity is always a myth. Even the Indiana Amish were in disagreement as to how to respond to the bishop's arrest. When the newspaper accounts appeared, representatives of the neighboring LaGrange Amish community issued a prompt statement to the press indicating that its church did not approve of Hochstetler's treatment of Lucy, nor did it believe that the authority accorded to the title of bishop pertained to actions in a clergyman's own home.[14] After his parole, some in the bishop's own Amish church wondered if he should retain his title.

Moreover, I believe that there are other, special temptations in writing as "we" on behalf of minority communities. Keeping the bittersweet memories of past trespasses alive may blind writers to immediate injustice or prevent us from appreciating the privileged positions we now hold. Writing as "we" can blind authors to the specific, the individual, the singular, the silent Lucy in any place or any time and may prevent the writer from admitting the Lucy within herself. In the latter half of the twentieth century, the ethnic narrative, the gendered narrative, and the political narrative were often framed as stories of victimization or survival. In this climate, "we" may be figured as Lucy, entitled to a certain authority because of past suffering, but this distortion remains a distortion of the singular story. Perhaps simple forms of authority are useful, and sometimes even unavoidable, for bosses, clergy, and official historians and political activists—those for whom the story of the group or institution must seem more important than the story of the individual—but they are not the authority of the writer.

The authority of the poet, as described by Evan Boland, is otherwise: "Paradoxically that authority grows the more the speaker is weakened and made vulnerable by the tensions he or she creates. By the same logic, it is diminished if the speaker protects himself or herself by the powers of language he or she can generate." The speaker must be at the same risk as all other elements in the text, not omniscient, not all-powerful.[15] And this position places the reader at risk as well. I think of my student at Messiah College who bravely articulated her own perplexity at finding herself in sympathy and identifying with a violent prisoner in a poem by Etheridge Knight, although she knew that in the world outside of the poem, she would not speak to or approve of such a person. The true poem forces an imaginative reach, and thereby it unsettles, scrambles categories, unnerves. To make another variation on an old theme: No disturbance for the writer, no disturbance for the reader.

If I have learned anything in recent years, it must be this: my own body struggling to articulate its experience is the voiceless body that most compels me to write.

CAMP HILL, 1997

IV

CONCLUSION

Others were tortured, refusing to accept release, in order to obtain a better resurrection. Others suffered mocking and flogging, and even chains and imprisonment. They were stoned to death, they were sawn in two, they were killed by the sword; they went about in skins of sheep and goats, destitute, persecuted, tormented—of whom the world was not worthy. They wandered in deserts and mountains, and in caves and holes in the ground.

Hebrews 11:35–38 (NRSV Inclusive Version)

Writing Like a Mennonite

10 Long ago someone called Mennonites *die Stillen im Lande* (the quiet in the land), a phrase that conveys the sense of a silent and defenseless community set against a noisy, violent world—and, at least for some, the name stuck. The phrase probably comes from Psalm 35:20, which is a complaint against an articulate enemy who uses language to persecute voiceless pacifists: "For they do not speak peace, but they conceive deceitful words against those who are quiet in the land" (NRSV). Until the traditional Anabaptist principles of nonresistance and community led some Mennonite people to become engaged with the antiwar and civil rights movements of the 1960s, Mennonites considered silence to be an appropriate attitude toward the wider world and a necessary means of survival in it—whether they inhabited deeply rooted farm communities in Pennsylvania or endured migrations across Europe or between the Americas. This attitude was borne of actual experience: Anabaptist migrant groups in Europe were often allowed to settle in new areas only if they promised not to proselytize or testify to their beliefs. They could live on the land as long as they remained quiet. In early America, a similar habit persisted.

Silence and seclusion became a strategy of living peaceably with the wider world as well as a means of keeping peace within the community. In the Pennsylvania Amish-Mennonite ethos I know, seductive and eloquent discourse was distrusted and considered a possible form of coercion. The choices a person made in daily life wrote the text that mattered most. Conflicts in family or community seemed to be smothered in silence, and because disturbing or minority views were rarely expressed in public, they could exist in their own quiet space on the margins, a kind of "don't ask, don't tell" policy for differences of many kinds. If deviant members refused to keep quiet, conflict could be fractious and bitter. In *Disquiet in the Land: Cultural Conflict in American Mennonite Communities,* Fred Kniss catalogues 208 examples of quarrels over issues ranging from the implementation of Sunday schools and participation in military service, to dress and language use in Mennonite Church communities in four eastern states between 1870 and 1985.[1] He concludes that conflicts often spring from two competing impulses in Mennonite life and thought: traditionalism, with its emphasis on moral, biblical, and collective authority; and communalism, expressed by pacifism, concern for justice, congregationalism, and mutual aid. A vivid example of this tension can be seen in current debates about how to respond to churches that openly accept gay and lesbian members: traditionalists opt for expulsion and excommunication, while some communalists argue for dialogue or even inclusion. Whereas schism can tear a community limb from limb and leave lasting scars for decades, at least it provides a means for both groups of people to disagree and still retain their sense of belonging to a fragment of the original community. For an individual, the cost of articulating a dissenting view is much greater. Rather than stir up trouble, draw unnecessary attention to themselves, or risk ostracism, individuals—especially if they were women—have often chosen to keep their most troubling thoughts to themselves.

I have another, more visceral sense of silence. I am still a child—at seven, at ten, and at fifteen—walking home from the school bus. The kindly grandfather figure of the neighborhood waves to me as he does every day, that gesture not so much a greeting as a way to lure me to his porch. Most days I resist, wave sweetly, and keep walking up the hill toward home as if I do not understand his desire. I am torn between not wanting to visit him and wanting to be good and obedient to a grown-up whom my family respects. So other days I comply, as I do this day. He leads me through the screen door to steps that descend to the cellar, where he will show me an elaborate miniature railroad set up for Christmas or a lathe where he turns wooden candleholders or the workbench where he grows seedlings each spring. Then he will pin me against a wall and stab his tongue against my teeth, which will be clenched tight, as I try to breathe. His tongue will taste sweet from chewing tobacco; his breath will heave as he presses his body against mine. I will never open my mouth to speak or scream, because I think that if I open my mouth his tongue will shoot down my throat like a snake.

Experience comes to a child simply, literally; only much later does it burst on me as a metaphor that has structured my thought and influenced my perceptions all these years. Now I wonder whether my quiet ancestors kept their mouths clamped shut for fear that another's tongue would plunge down their throats. Is this why the shift from oral German dialects to English or Russian or Spanish or Portuguese has always been so painful in Mennonite communities and families? I wonder if a memory of trauma and fear of violation has kept Mennonites from producing imaginative literature until recently, even though they have been living in literate and safely landed communities in America since colonial times. John Ruth has recounted many other reasons for our failure to write in times past: a legacy of iconoclasm from the Radical Reformation, a distrust of the assimilating influence of education and high culture, a devaluation of the individual voice in the service of the collective religious community, a deep commitment to facts and plain speech, and the folk culture's underlying values of practicality, hard work, and thrift.[2] Nevertheless, as plain dress, a strange dialect, and the geographical separation of valleys or remote prairie villages have delineated safety zones for vulnerable Mennonite bodies in times past, so the absence of literary activity has hidden Mennonite hearts and minds from the curious gaze of others. In the absence of published fiction and poetry, outsiders have no access to the experience and imagination of the community. Perhaps the refusal of previous generations to publish imaginative work was another kind of cultural resistance, borne of distrust and of a fear that literature would somehow expose the interior life of the community—or of the individual—and thereby make them vulnerable to violation.

When the man was done, I would let his wood-framed cellar door slam shut and walk home through the backyards, thinking, "Well, that was not so bad. It was only my body." I think that the martyr stories taught me that wonderful splintering trick: it is only the body. In one of my favorite engravings, it is only the body of Anneken Hendriks tied to a ladder that forever tips headfirst into a fire of the Spanish Inquisition, her hands pressed together in prayer. In another story, Maeyken Wens knows it is only a body that her children will miss after she burns at the stake, her tongue clamped so that she cannot speak. "Fear not them which kill the body," it says in Maeyken's section of the *Martyrs' Mirror*, paraphrasing Matthew 10:28: "And fear not them which kill the body but are not able to kill the soul; but rather fear him which is able to destroy both soul and body in hell."[3] They can burn the body but not the soul. You may gaze at my body, even touch it if you must, but you will not know my soul: my essential self exists safely apart from my body and from you. Therapists call this splintering of consciousness "dissociation" and count it among the common psychological strategies employed by those who survive physical trauma.

Once, after a reading I gave from *Eve's Striptease*, a tall, distinguished-looking woman with silvery hair approached me and simply said, "I had an experience like yours, but I do not speak of it. I stand on my silence." And she seemed to have found solid ground to stand on. Rather than endure the feelings of violation that invariably accom-

Anneken Hendriks, Amsterdam, 1571. Jan Luyken etching.

pany revelation of childhood sexual mistreatment, she chose to keep a dignified silence. Although sometimes mistaken for compliance, the refusal to speak in defense of oneself can be a fierce form of resistance, as when Jesus refused to speak before Pilot or when he hung on the cross and "opened not his mouth . . . as a sheep before her shearers is dumb" (Isaiah 53:7). Certainly this stance has helped to consolidate identity and has served as a means of resistance for Mennonites; silence is a worthy weapon for a pacifist body that carries memories of physical violation. Following the literal teachings of Jesus, Mennonites have refused for centuries to defend themselves with any sort of visible force—including the force of language in legal courts.

When two thieves approached the end of a wharf off Manhattan's west side where I was sitting with my writer friend Donald, my first thought was not to speak or fight but to flee, leaving him behind. Approaching a couple of men down the pier, I could find no words to explain what was happening to us or why I wanted to stand there with them, mute as I was. Meanwhile, because Donald had no money, the thieves came for me, and the two men nearby scattered, confused and sensing trouble. While the male thief held Donald, his female partner shoved my shoulders and chest, but I refused to give up the seven dollars in my purse. I was sure that only fingers poked in their coat pockets, not guns. Exasperated, Donald finally convinced me to give them whatever was in my wallet, and then they sprinted toward shore, where a police car happened to be cruising by. Donald ran after them and hopped into the back of one of the police cars, which took off in pursuit of the thieves. I remained behind on the pier, and a kind man named Gabriel, who had witnessed the chase, stayed with me until the police returned. In parting, he asked me to be sure to testify against the thieves if they were apprehended. Drug addicts often robbed gay men in that neighborhood, he explained, and the cops were rarely sympathetic.

Later, at the station house, the policemen assured me that my testimony would send the man, who was on parole, "up the river" to a penitentiary for several years because his pretend pistol elevated the theft to a felony. During the next few days I searched for alternatives, but it was nearly impossible to make the city's victim services workers understand that I was unsure about whether to testify against my predator. I had no memory of my parents ever talking to the police; it just seemed to be something we don't do. The more I dealt with the criminal justice system, whose workers were unguardedly bigoted, the more deeply I identified with the African-American man and his female accomplice who had escaped. The assistant district attorney explained that the decision to press charges was the state's, not mine, and threatened to subpoena my testimony.

My conscience remained unsettled until the morning I phoned a Mennonite acquaintance who worked as a chaplain at the city's prison on Riker's Island. In a voice still blurry with sleep, he suggested that my refusing to testify might be the worst form of pride: taking responsibility for another's choice. It may be an especially Mennonite temptation to assume that we can make peace in the world by absorbing its violence onto our own bodies. His advice resonated with my memories from a Mennonite college in the early 1980s, when a couple of my classmates who had refused to register for the draft faced criminal charges, and one Anabaptist leader suggested that North American boys could make peace by actually placing their bodies between military lines in El Salvador.

In the end, I testified before a grand jury, and the case was later settled without trial. Leaving the courthouse that clear autumn afternoon, I was swept with a surprising sense of relief. It seemed impossible that all I had to do was just to say what had happened. I hadn't expected the jurors to believe my story, so I wore the most innocent floral print church dress in my closet. Partly I had blamed myself for the mugging, as if two writers out on a pier watching the sun go down over New Jersey somehow deserved to be punished. Indeed, most New Yorkers gave me that sense, as they instantly asked, "What were you doing out there at dusk?" (That placing of blame on the victim is urban magical thinking that traces effect to cause and thereby allows the speaker to distance himself from the episode, believing that he is safe from random acts of violence.) I didn't tell my parents about the robbery until long afterward, not wanting to worry them or confirm a sense that my home was unsafe.

Nonetheless, walking away from the court room into Chinatown's chaotic streets, I felt oddly light and shaken. The secret I carried from childhood remained buried, but I now know that it must have been tangled up in my heady sense of relief. I had simply said what happened to me, and I had been believed, not blamed. I'd even heard one of the jurors let out a moan of sympathy and exasperation when I told the prosecutor how much money was in my purse. On the way back to my office, I stopped to watch a worker release garments from the window of a third-story sweatshop. Red silk blouses on hangers gracefully glided down a line to a man loading a truck below, scarlet tongues flapping in the wind.

Stranger than my sense of relief that day is the fact that the robbery took place several hours after I learned that my first book would be published. Donald's first novel also found a publisher later that year, and ever since then, we have referred to book publications as "muggings." It is impossible to prepare for the sudden terror and vulnerability that comes with the news that one's thoughts will become print.

Even when a book is consciously written with that goal in mind, the event of publication can feel like a violation—especially to authors who are driven to write because their tongues are somehow tied. Until the publication of *Sleeping Preacher,* I had been content to confide my ideas about family, history, and Mennonite culture to a notebook page. But on the Tuesday after Labor Day in 1991, a morning phone call from the University of Pittsburgh Press and an evening robbery made it impossible for me to remain silent—in several senses.

A poem included in that first collection revealed to my family for the first time what had occurred in the home of that elderly neighbor man. My parents' concern about raising us away from the traditional community had been soothed by kind neighbors like him—a Mason, not a Mennonite, yet every bit as generous and kind to my brothers and me as a grandfather might have been. For two decades my silence had protected them and also had protected him. Growing up, I had simply absorbed his assault on my spirit and body and had hidden my knowledge away in some secret place. I wanted to disturb no one. Perhaps even then I sensed that, for my parents, the choice to raise children away from their community of origin was a risk. My silence supported their hope that life is more complex than the dualism that would divide experience between the safety of the sect and the danger of the world. Indeed, within that one man I knew both kindness and coercion, a contradiction that to this day I cannot explain and must simply accept. Several times in college I had tried to write about it— once as a poem, once as a narrative sketch—but both pieces remained undeveloped. It was not until the summer I was twenty-six, at the MacDowell artists' colony in New Hampshire for the first time, that I wrote "The Interesting Thing," a poem I included in my book.

To bring this kind of information to light, even in writing, is never simple. When an ancient violation is finally named, people are at a loss about what to do: what to remember and what to forget, whether there is any way to make amends, or whether retribution will only continue a cycle of violation. It is difficult to know what brings healing and justice. At the personal level, these questions are complex. At

THE INTERESTING THING

The interesting thing is not that a boy
could cut off the head of a doll with a toy
saw. The interesting thing is that the parents
would blame the girl, because she had a new baby brother.
The interesting thing is not that the brother
would hang a plastic baby from a limb
and tie his sister to the trunk beneath it,
her ankles and wrists burned by rope, but that,
when found, she would insist,
"A neighbor did this." The thing is not
that an old neighbor would wave the girl in
on her way home from school to show her
seedlings sprouting under a violet Gro-Lux light
in his basement, not that he would wheeze
in her ear, or even that he would stab
his tobacco-sweet tongue against her teeth,
but that the girl would walk home,
spitting out the taste of him
and tell no one.

the local and national level, I see them everywhere as my mind's eye moves down the cities of the Eastern Seaboard to the American South, from Haiti to South America, across the ocean to Western Europe and the former Soviet Union and the Balkans, down the coast and around the cape of South Africa, up to the Middle East and across the subcontinent of India and Pakistan, across Burma to Cambodia, Vietnam, and the People's Republic of China. If it is impossible to correct the horrible things that people have done to one another, then why even try? Consider the recent Japanese apology to Korean women pressed into prostitution during World War II or the rehabilitation of the victims of the 1692 Salem witch trials in New England. Do these gestures offer any critique of history's cruel cycles of violence? Do they prevent future abuses? Yet the cost of not remembering and telling those stories—at least for me—is the unconscious repetition of violence, on the self and onto others.

One evening, after a day of solitary work at MacDowell, I was sitting at a small bar table with three other writers from the artists' colony, listening as one told how he had gotten expelled from Brooklyn College in the 1960s for publishing an underground newspaper. Although I don't like to smoke, I had a cigarette in my hand when one of the men asked the storyteller, "Why did they kick you out—for printing the word *cunt*?" The force of that word caused me to swiftly reach across the table and press my smoldering cigarette into the speaker's chest. "Jesus, Mary, and Joseph!" the Irish poet cursed. The rest of us froze, silent, until someone finally said, "Any man can go to a colony and have an affair, but how many men get burned with a cigarette?"

That he would link violence with sex through some vague association of excess in that moment is incisive. In a situation where I was surrounded by older and more accomplished male authors, I took up a cigarette—shape of a pen, shape of a penis—and burned a man's body because he had uttered the word that names and degrades female difference. The myth of female castration—that women are only castrated men, males without potency—is as powerfully embedded in Western culture as Oedipus, Angela Carter reminds us. This myth, which supports erotic violence and male domination, is "an imaginary fact that pervades the whole of men's attitude towards women and our attitude to ourselves, that transforms women from human beings into wounded creatures who are born to bleed."[4]

The next morning the Irish poet appeared at breakfast with a salved wound the size of a dime shining angry red where his shirt hung open. He needed to speak with me, he said. He needed to know why I had done it. I hardly knew him, so how could I have known that he wouldn't hurt me in response to such a reckless deed? I told him that I was sorry, terribly sorry, but in fact I felt only surprise at my capacity to enact that cliché of contemporary torturers. Although we have remained on good terms through the years, the poor man had to explain the episode to himself in the end, writing a villanelle called, "What Does it Mean to be Touched by Fire?" The end rhymes that I recall—fire, desire, conspire—all suggest pain, sex, and collusion.

It would take many years for me to begin to see the ways that violence is linked not only to sex but also to writing. Writing is a process by which suppressed feelings come to consciousness, sometimes painfully. I believe that it is no coincidence that I committed an act both cruel and erotic—at least in some metaphoric sense—when I was just beginning to write out of my own memories of trauma. It is as though I had swallowed a hook long ago and the force with which I was tugging at the line to pull memory loose from my flesh caused me to lash out with a monstrous, unconscious gesture. As the mugging painfully forced me to speak on my own behalf, so childhood violation was gradually pushing me toward articulation, the way a splinter will work its way to the skin's surface, festering, trying to heal. The wound becomes a mouth that finally speaks its testimony, thereby transforming a mute, confused victim into a subject with a clear vision of her experience and a literate voice.

II

That trauma can both confine one to silence and compel one to find articulation is clear in the brief history of Mennonite literature. Apart from some devotional books, the first, and by far most important work by Mennonite authors is *The Bloody Theater or Martyrs Mirror of the Defenseless Christians Who Baptized Only Upon Confession of Faith, and Who Suffered and Died for the Testimony of Jesus, Their Savior, from the Time of Christ to the Year A. D. 1660.* First published in 1660 in an edition of 1,000 copies, this enormous book contains texts composed by or about individuals enduring torture, on trial, or awaiting execution. Commonly called only *Martyrs Mirror,* the book's full title is useful for the way it defines the words *Anabaptist*—a Christian pacifist who practices adult baptism—and *martyr*—one who dies testifying for beliefs. Elsewhere much has been made of the way this title underlines the spectacle of martyrdom, which unfolded in public, according to a civil and religious script.[5] Yet the word which interests me most is *testimony.*

In cases where court records are preserved, the "testimony" of the martyrs in this book is quite literal. Yet all of the 4,011 "died for the testimony of Jesus." In some cases, their testimony is preserved in letters and verse written to relatives and fellow believers. For illiterate people, martyrdom itself became a kind of writing with the body, because the martyrs' words and actions were converted into textual form as a consequence of the physical ordeals they chose to endure. For Anabaptist sisters, martyrdom represented a choice to enact the ultimate sacrifice that placed them on equal ground with their brethren. A third or more of the sixteenth-century martyrs were women, and in some regions during the worst periods of persecution, as many as four in ten of the martyrs were female.[6] For instance, Annekin Hendriks is described in *Martyrs Mirror* as Anneken de Vlaster, a housewife from Frisia who could neither read nor write. Yet her dramatic death in Amsterdam in October of 1571 ensured that her words were inscribed forever. The fifty-three-year-old woman, who probably worked as a linen weaver, was so loud and verbal about her faith that the authorities stuffed her mouth with gunpowder to keep her from giving "good witness" to spectators at her execution. The account does not say whether her skull mercifully exploded when her ladder-bound body fell into the flames, but we know that she did not silently store her convictions there. Her words and courage inspired Dutch Mennonites to write a hymn that narrates her execution. In addition, fifty-three hymn texts were written by imprisoned Anabaptists awaiting execution and preserved in the *Ausbund,* a 1564 worship book still used by the Amish.

Even after the Anabaptist era, trauma continued to be a means of articulation and inscription at those times when it did not silence the community altogether. Whereas the Mennonites and Amish who migrated to America during the colonial period published next to no literature for a broader audience until well after World War II, those who had migrated to colonies in Russia during the eighteenth century did publish, but mostly after their communities were destroyed. "The tragic upheaval of war and revolution and the destruction of the Mennonite commonwealth in Russia shocked the Mennonite literary imagination into life as nothing had since the age of martyrdom," observed Al Reimer in a 1993 survey of North American Mennonite writing.[7] During the 1920s and 1930s, a few émigré authors, mostly located in the Canadian West, tried to make sense of that traumatic loss by writing and publishing literature, often in *Plautdietsch,* the German-based mother tongue of their Russian childhoods. Like other literatures of loss—Isaac Bashevis Singer's Yiddish novels come to mind—this work preserved the memory of an ethnic homeland, often portrayed as Edenic.

In these literary efforts, and through countless oral repetitions of violence and dislocation narratives that are still repeated in Mennonite communities, I see spontaneous attempts by individuals to heal the consequences of trauma. From the time of Freud's first work with hysterics, and from early research into shell-shock, the inability to speak has been associated with trauma. Almost from the start, doctors believed that the physioneurosis caused by terror could be reversed with words. It seems that while normal memory exists in narrative structures, the memories of trauma lack context or language and persist only as vivid sensations or images. If these memories and feelings can be articulated and shaped into narrative form, they can thereby be integrated into the rest of a life's experience. A 1992 study by Harvard physician Judith Herman links research into private traumas such as domestic violence and public traumas such as terrorism. Herman relates current work with torture survivors in Chile, where therapists have helped victims to write detailed narrative accounts of their mistreatment and then to relive the experiences by speaking them within a supportive community. "The action of telling a story in the safety of a protected relationship can actually produce a change in the abnormal processing of the traumatic memory," she writes.[8] I wonder whether *Martyrs Mirror* has sometimes served this purpose at a collective level, for it seems that the book was most often printed in conjunction with an impending war, the need for stories felt most keenly in relation to the community's fresh fears of persecution.

It would also follow that in those times when the community has refused to hear traumatic stories, it has hindered healing. I think of the Mennonites who remained in Soviet Russia after the 1920s migrations and who therefore faced the brutalities of Stalin's regime: collectivization, cultural and religious repression, and the systematic deportation or execution of most able-bodied men. By 1941, the invasion of the German army enabled these Mennonite villages, dominated by women then, to open their churches and conduct school in their own language. For a time, the occupying troops took Mennonite women to be their translators, assistants, and mistresses. When the German army began to retreat in 1943, German-speaking people followed the army in a trek toward Germany, certain they would be killed if they did not stay ahead of advancing Russian troops. A number of these women—some with children, some widowed, some separated from husbands who had been deported to labor camps—emigrated to Mennonite communities in Canada. Although many of these women were eventually integrated into the Canadian communities, they were not warmly received on their arrival after the war. Because of their dubious marital status, many were denied membership in Mennonite churches, and no one wanted to listen to their stories of violence, combat, sexual assault, or impropriety. A desire for peace and purity prevented the community from helping these women to heal, their trauma compounded by abandonment and isolation in an era when common wisdom advised survivors to forget the past and count their blessings. Even now, as full members of the community, most of these women have chosen not to speak about their experiences of war or their initial encounters with Canadian Mennonites.

In 1994 Pamela Klassen published a powerful ethnographic study based on the stories of two of these women.[9] Oddly enough, I first read this book while waiting to be called for jury duty, sitting on a mahogany pew in the massive main hall of Brooklyn's criminal court. I was so moved by the tragedy of the women's experience and Klassen's skillful analysis that I wept, my body curled over the paperback, in the din of that chaotic public space. When my name was called to sit for a lawsuit, I told the attorneys that I come from a Mennonite background, and they dismissed me from the case immediately, knowing of the sect's reputation for being nonlitigious, noncooperative, and apart from civil society.

A serious work of literature by a Mennonite critiquing Mennonite experience was not published for broad distribution in a language that could be understood by the dominant culture until Rudy Wiebe's *Peace Shall Destroy Many* appeared in 1962—this was 302 years after the *Martyrs Mirror* was published in the Netherlands for readers of Dutch.[10] When this book appeared, Wiebe received a letter from B. B. Janz, the venerable church leader who had negotiated with authorities for two years to arrange the 1923 migration of Mennonites from Russia to Canada. In his fine Gothic German hand, Janz asked Wiebe why he would publish a book in the English language that cast the Mennonite settlers in such an unflattering light. His chief concern was grave: if images such as these were broadly available, and if the Canadians decided that they could no longer offer a home to Mennonites, where in the world would they ever find another place to live?

Subsequently, and especially in recent years, Mennonite writers have proliferated and flourished like prairie grasses in the Canadian West, where they are often celebrated as pioneering rebel-heroes. If they are vulnerable at all, the terror comes from an internalized threat. Poet Di Brandt has said that she believed Mennonites from her farm village would kill her if she published her first book of poems, *questions i asked my mother*. Can she actually mean that Low German–speaking farmers from Rhineland, Manitoba, would find her house in Winnipeg or Windsor and knock on her door in the night, stamping their dung-clotted boots on her porch? Do they carry shotguns or pitchforks in her imagination, I wonder? The frequency with which she has mentioned this fear in public—once in a reading that I heard in 1990, three times in her 1995 collection of essays, *Dancing Naked*—

suggests that it must be true in some sense, however unlikely in another. Her fear contains the truth of myth. Because she seized the authority of literature and persecuted her community by telling its secrets and exposing its shame, it must punish her in turn—as happened after Rudy Wiebe's first novel, as happened to the martyrs of old.

Before the publication of *Sleeping Preacher,* I also dreaded my book's reception in the Mennonite community, although it turned out to be warmer than I ever imagined. Given my context, perhaps I needed to imagine punishment in order to cast myself in the position of author. This reminds me of a short but famous essay by Michel Foucault in which he traces the evolution of contemporary notions of authorship. Long before copyright designated the individual ownership of texts, he writes, the name of an actual author—not the name of the king or of a religious or mythic figure—was ascribed to a text only when it was considered transgressive and subject to censorship and punishment. Writing was regarded as an act fraught with risk, enacted on a field defined by the opposing poles of sacred or profane, lawful or unlawful.[11] I am not prepared to evaluate this idea in terms of historical fact, but its truth as a myth seems clear enough, and I would add to Foucault's list of oppositions, another: those ideas that are supportive of the community and those that are threatening to it. Moreover, I have noticed that, within the community, those writers who are regarded as transgressive seem to be taken most seriously by their Mennonite readers, as if the vague threat of punishment were a mark of authenticity or excellence. The terror of punishment for Mennonite writers—whether real or imagined—seems to invigorate creativity as persecution and trauma engendered Mennonite literature longer ago. "The more ye mow us down, the more we grow," wrote the second-century church father Tertullian. "The blood of the martyrs is the seed of the church."[12]

I have begun to question the disturbing consequences of this martyr identity, however, with the assistance of Lois Frey, a Mennonite-turned-Quaker therapist who has studied creativity and trauma for

FIRST BIRD

The first bird that sings
sings for all birds, even

when she stands for nothing
but herself, a dun-colored finch

on a dogwood branch.
No telling what a bird knows,

if this seems the first time
light glowed on the horizon,

or if she thinks her beak
alone has pierced the night.

We know nothing can be whole
that hasn't been torn.

There is no holy thing
that hasn't been betrayed,

the way notes, once forced
into her tiny throat,

come out this dawn as song.

more than twenty years. She believes that trauma either destroys creativity by making a child too afraid to risk new experiences; or, if it is not so overwhelming, trauma may enable a child to grow, both in strength and in creativity, through the various ways she finds of mastering her injury. Frey wonders what causes a child to turn in either of these opposite directions, and a few years ago she turned her attention to Mennonites, whom she believes have inherited "encapsulated trauma." Symptoms of this inheritance that she recognizes in the Mennonite culture of her childhood include splitting of the self, impaired capacity for fantasy and symbolization, literal and concrete thinking, defensive occupation with the mundane, and memory behaviors that tend to repeat the trauma. The response to a memory of trauma is the curtailing of creativity and a self-protective and fearful refusal to take risks. Cautious behaviors that once protected endangered beings thereby "retraumatize" them.

One aspect of the Mennonite inheritance Frey has named the "persecutor/martyr introject." *Introjection* is a process whereby things from the world—actual persecutors and martyrs, for instance—become embedded in the unconscious as a pattern of behavior persisting for generations. Among Mennonites, Frey believes, a collective history of victimization, social ostracism, and persecution has written a persecutor/martyr script that gets replayed within the community or within a family every time an individual is censored or marginalized. To break beyond the victim/perpetrator introject, one must integrate both identities within the self. Confronting experience through the production of art is one means of escaping the scripted, narrow roles of victim and perpetrator. Moreover, an artwork's ability to express ambiguity and paradox enables an individual to recognize that she is capable of playing both roles. The production of artistic works thus enables a person to integrate the opposite identities into a whole and complex personality capable of confident, public expression.[13]

In many respects, I agree with Frey's assertions, but I am uneasy about the large claims they make for artistic work. It may appear in her public performance that the poet has become confident and capable; the voice in the poem or on stage seems to have mastered the injury— at once immersed in it and in control of it. Louise Glück brilliantly recounts this apparent "revenge on circumstance": "For a brief period, the natural arrangement is reversed: the artist no longer acted upon but acting; the last word, for the moment, seized back from fate or chance. Control of the past: as though the dead martyrs were to stand up in the arena and say, 'Suppose, on the other hand . . .' No process I can name so completely defeats the authority of event."[14]

Of course, this triumphal moment exists only within the process of writing and within the written text. This is because writing enables the author to transcend the limits of her body and to evade the demands that others may place upon her. A written text cannot be made to change in response to others; it does not fail to speak out of fear, nor can it alter in response to the loving attention of a reader. Moreover, it exists in a time and in a space quite apart from the body of its author. Unbeknownst to me, you read this book, for instance; even after my death, it will exist. Although much is made of the "writer's voice," text is not speech. In fact, as the ultimate disconnection from the life world, the ultimate dissociation, writing may be the most brilliant splintering trick of all. It has taken me some time to grasp the fact that, in this way, my cure has also been my curse.

This split is another way that writing may be bound to violence. In order to write, an author gives up her conversations with the world, withdrawing for a time from the company of those she loves and from the pleasures and pains of living. French novelist, playwright, and mother Hêlêne Cixous admits, "Between the writer and his or her family the question is always one of departing while remaining present, of being absent while in full presence, of escaping, of abandon. It is both utterly banal and the thing we don't want to know or say. A writer has no children; I have no children when I write."[15]

I think of Maeyken Wens, most disturbing to me of the Anabaptist martyrs because her story glorifies a choice to abandon her children rather than recant. Could she not have practiced some form of the splintering trick: comply with the authorities yet still believe whatever she wanted in silence, for the sake of her sons? As much as I want to argue for the heroic voice, I also regret her choice, unable to imagine what it must have meant in her time. Maeyken Wens's letters to her family are preserved in the *Martyrs Mirror,* but most startling is the written narrative of fifteen-year-old Adriaen. Standing with three-year-old Hans on his arm to witness their mother's execution, Adriaen fainted and only revived when the fire had burned to a smoking heap. Searching the coals of his mother's execution fire, Adriaen found the contraption made of two blades that were screwed together to secure her tongue. Today this relic remains in the possession of Dutch Mennonites in Amsterdam, a phallic-shaped symbol of brutal force and silence, which, like the cross, is transformed by tradition into a beloved emblem of sacrifice and witness. The engraving in *Martyrs Mirror* shows, not the martyr Maeyken, but an almost comical view of Adriaen's broad behind as he reaches for the tongue screw in the smoldering coals, while Hans, still wearing a baby's dress, looks on.

In an essay about the staggering numbers of Christian martyrs who, during the twentieth century, suffered under regimes on all points of

The children of Maeyken Wens, Antwerp, 1573. Jan Luyken etching.

the political spectrum, poet Dana Gioia reveals an etymological fact that I find very interesting. Historically, the word *martyr* carries no trace of suffering or death. Its root means only "witness"—witness to a truth. "The martyr's task is not armed resistance; nor is it even passive suffering," Gioia writes. "Persecution and death are only the by-products of the martyr's true role—to witness the truth uncompromised."[16]

For many people, the deathbed is the only place where they finally can bear to reveal the truths they have silently carried all of their lives. Facing death, they are finally free to speak with the clarity of those Anabaptist martyrs who gave "good witness" when facing the flames of an executioner's fire. Hêlêne Cixous identifies death—or an awareness of mortality—as the first rung on the ladder of writing.[17] This is the ladder, tipping toward the fire, on which Anneken Hendriks was bound. The author must lean into the scorching truth of her own mortality in order to write. She must write the book that threatens to cost her her life.

The implications of the martyr's example are absolute: one must bear witness to the only truth one sees. It is a matter of consequence that the word *witness* means not only "to see," but also "to speak." To write like a martyr means, not to choose death, but to choose to bear life-giving witness, to communicate the truth of one's own vision or insight, to affirm its value with confidence, no matter how arrogant or disturbing it may be, "and the truth shall make you free" (John 8:32). When my poem about the old neighbor was finally published, it shattered my family's perceptions of a person whom they had known to be only benevolent and generous. That is a violent act. No wonder the one who disturbs a perceived truth is felt to be an aggressor.

I also know that, by speaking of that molestation, I risk becoming defined and marked by its shame. But how different is that experience from any unfortunate thing that happens to a child on her way to becoming an adult? It may be no different, except in the scope of its consequences, from what happened to me at the age of twelve, while hiking a mountain trail at church camp, when a copperhead bite transformed me from a child who could catch garter snakes with her brothers into a child with recurring nightmares of a floor so thick with serpents that it undulated; of copperheads so smart they could read my mind, which was plotting an escape; of snakes that turned and attacked when I opened my mouth to cry for help and no sound came out. Even now, terror rushes through my body whenever a snake flashes on the television screen or I see a patch of snake skin slither under the leaves in my garden. Metaphoric associations aside, does the snake bite brand me in the eyes of my readers any less than the touch of an old man? Or does everything always and only collapse into the shapes of familiar narrative plots?

III   As a community carries memories of trauma, so does an individual's body, often accompanied by deep and contradictory desires to deny and declare the pain.[18] As a little girl, I found in the martyr stories a way to survive: It is only my body you can touch. The split between body and spirit that I learned in such a visceral way exactly parallels the split between experience and words that developed centuries ago with the technology of writing. The disembodied medium of letters has enabled me to loosen from my body's recesses those old wounds, to re-create them on a page, and, eventually, to speak. Yet whatever I learned from my own texts, whatever I am able to say there, is only partial if I cannot also speak with others. "Writing is the only cure," an old maxim says, and I used to believe this, until I realized that writing was only part of a long training for the day when I would be able to talk. I bore on my body a violence until I could write; I bore witness in writing until I could speak.

Among the few material objects I have from that old neighbor man is a huge 1927 unabridged dictionary with elaborate Art Deco ornaments on its spine. On the title page are these words, inscribed in his inky cursive:

> *This book is my pride and joy*
> *Presented to Julia Spicher*
> *Dec. 6, 1980*
> *Remember me.*

It was a gift for my seventeenth birthday. By then I had been scribbling in school tablets for years, writing to make sense of the fragmented and silent parts of my life, removing language from my own body and inscribing it on that safe, quiet space of the page, where I could assemble and view it again. When he gave me that gift with its heartfelt inscription to remember him, did he assume that I would also remain quiet about the liberties he had taken with my body for a decade? That secret may have been more damaging than the touch of a pedophile's hand for the ways it has gagged my mouth and bound my body, isolating me in silence. Did he think I would fail to remember myself?

The tight-lipped survival strategy of my childhood is no longer useful, and in the martyr stories, I now see, not submission and silence, but men and women who spoke with their words and with their bodies, who refused to hold their tongues or keep the peace. Although I have succumbed to both temptations, I now write not for revenge—following popular tales of victim and monster—nor for redemption—following a Christian paradigm that is often too swift to be true. Following my perpetrator's advice, I write simply to remember and to bear witness.

The meaning of the word *memory* for me is enriched when I see that its tangled Indo-European roots run through the Latin *memor* (mindful); the Greek *martus* (witness), which became *martyr;* as well as the Germanic and Old English *murnam* (to grieve). We write to bring things in mind, to witness, and eventually, to grieve. Thus, I learn to refuse the abusive one within myself who will always beckon me back into that house. Though I may be tempted to be nice and comply, how can I return to that hushed place, when I would rather stay out on the road, offering myself to conversation and relationship as a martyr offers her body to flames? I must find my own life's pleasures, unable to recant or let some other tongue go down my throat.

CAMP HILL, 2000

Afterword

I once heard John Ruth tell the story of a preacher in Eastern Pennsylvania who, during the wrenching language shift of the nineteenth century, stood up to preach his first sermon in English. When he opened his mouth, only a great wail came out, and the poor man stood there, gripping the edges of the pulpit, sobbing, voiceless and torn. Ruth said he believes that in times of change and stress some individuals in a community just act the way lightning rods work on barn roofs. The tension of cultural shift gathers and concentrates until a great vein forms and finally strikes someone; the trouble finds its way to the ground. Maybe the true sleeping preachers of the nineteenth century were such individuals—their dissociative trance states the consequence of the trauma of congregational schism as the industrial revolution reached rural areas and the nation absorbed the spiritual implications of a civil war.

This summer, everywhere I go Mennonite people are talking about unity and fragmentation, often at the same time. As the two main bodies of the denomination within the United States plan to merge, some are predicting an immediate schism. The troublesome issue is the status of gay and lesbian members. As a painful war is waged over the bodies of homosexual people, I believe that this trouble expresses deeper anxieties about gender and the nature of family and sex. Two Mennonite colleges now have female presidents, while a large conference of the church has tabled for five years official discussions about the ordination of women. Divorce and remarriage are no longer unheard of in Mennonite homes, and heterosexual abuses are coming to light in some communities. This time of moral confusion leaves some with one comforting certainty—and the push to exclude gay and lesbian people is surely not limited to Mennonites. Also this summer, the U.S. Supreme Court supported the decision of the Boy Scouts to exclude gay people from their organization.

As I finish this book, I am more certain than ever of the need to resist coercion and violence against the body. Repression and denial are responses of entire societies as well as of individuals, and the struggle to speak out of silence on behalf of defenseless beings is the primary challenge of our time. Surely this value is bound to the ideals of my Anabaptist ancestors, who made enormous sacrifices in order to bear "good witness." Yet as I finish this book, I also feel its limits—the daunting permanence of print and the failures of my own perceptions.

This work has been hard on my body. Sometimes I wonder if I have made of this project a trial, the way those celibate men who labored down the road from here at Ephrata made a martyrdom of their labors over *Martyrs Mirror*. Most days now, I rise from the computer in my office at Messiah College aching. Perhaps pain is only an appropriate response to painful material, but it is late June, and the lawns surrounding Old Main are flush with orange day lilies, the kind that grow wild along back roads around here. Whenever I see them, a Bible verse learned by heart in childhood comes to mind: "Consider the lilies, how they grow: they toil not, they spin not; and yet I say unto you, that Solomon in all his glory was not arrayed like one of these" (Luke 12:27 KJV). I would like to consider the lilies. I would like to abandon this work, knowing that the words of the wisest poet of Hebrew antiquity can't compare with one of those brilliant blossoms, which opens at dawn and wilts by dusk. Though my view of these flowers is mediated through a text, I know that beyond the book, beyond the limits of the body, are healing mysteries that have nothing to do with labor or language.

In less than a month, I will take my books from these shelves, and David and I will move to Centre County, in the Ridge and Valley region, so that I may take a teaching position at Pennsylvania State University. As I finish this collection, it feels as if I am also closing a chapter of my life, drawing closer to the landscape and people of my origins even as I drift farther from its institutions.

CAMP HILL, 2000

Notes

2   Tracking the Mullein, or Portrait of a Mennonite Muse

1. Paul Erb, *We Believe* (Scottdale, Pa.: Herald Press, 1969), 63.

2. Hêlêne Cixous, *Three Steps on the Ladder of Writing* (New York: Columbia University Press, 1993), 11.

3. Salman Rushdie, "Imaginary Homelands," in *Imaginary Homelands: Essays and Criticism, 1981–1991* (London: Granta Books / Penguin, 1992), 12.

4. John Ruth to author, 13 September 1997.

5. Rachel A. Yoder Spicher, 1948 personal diaries, in possession of the author.

6. William A. Niering and Nancy C. Olmstead, *National Audubon Society Field Guide to North American Wildflowers: Eastern Region* (New York: Knopf, 1979), 798.

7. I am indebted to writer and amateur botanist Gabriel Welsch, who described the habits of the mullein to me.

8. Alastair Hamilton, S. Voolstra, Pe. Visser, eds., *From Martyr to Muppy: A Historical Introduction to Cultural Assimilation Processes of a Religious Minority in the Netherlands, the Mennonites* (Amsterdam: Amsterdam University Press, 1994), 78. I am grateful to Ervin Beck for pointing out this image in his paper, "The Signifying Menno: Archetypes for Authors and Critics," delivered at "Mennonite(s) Writing in the United States," 24–26 October 1997, Goshen, Ind. An English translation of "The Mennonite Sister" poem is found in *Mennonite Life* 10 (1995): 129–31.

9. William Carlos Williams, "A Sort of a Song," in *Selected Poems* (New York: New Directions, 1985), 145.

10. Robert Lowell, "91 Revere Street," in *Life Studies* (New York: Farrar, Straus & Giroux, 1956), 38–39.

3   When the Stranger Is an Angel

1. Zora Neale Hurston, *Their Eyes Were Watching God* (New York: Harper & Row / Perennial Library, 1990), 46.

2. For insights into the role of the stranger, I am indebted to Virginia Sha-batay's essay, "The Stranger's Story: Who Calls and Who Answers?" in Carol Witherell and Nel Noddings, *Stories Lives Tell: Narrative and Dialogue in Education* (New York: Columbia Teachers College Press, 1991), 136–52.

4 Bringing Home the Work

1. Quoted in Hildi Froese Tiessen, Introduction to *Liars and Rascals* (Water-loo, Ontario: University of Waterloo Press, 1989), xii.

2. *New York Times,* 14 October 1991, inset quotation, 1.

3. John Ruth, review of *Liars and Rascals,* ed. Hildi Froese Tiessen, in *Mennonite Reporter* (Canada), 28 June 1989, 11.

4. Levi Miller, review of *Liars and Rascals,* ed. Hildi Froese Tiessen, in *Festival Quarterly* (fall 1998): 29.

5 Preacher's Striptease

1. Unnamed reviewer, review of *Sleeping Preacher* by Julia Kasdorf, in *Publisher's Weekly,* 10 October 1992. Emily Grosholz, review of *Sleeping Preacher* by Julia Kasdorf, in *Hudson Review* (October 1993): 570.

2. John Berger, *Ways of Seeing* (London: BBC and Penguin, 1972), 54.

3. W. E. B. DuBois, from "Souls of Black Folk," in *The Oxford W. E. B. DuBois Reader,* ed. Eric J. Sundquist (New York: Oxford University Press, 1996), 102.

4. This poem appeared in *Mennonot,* September 1994, 10; used with permission.

5. Jeff Gundy, "U.S. Mennonite Poetry and Poets: Beyond Dr. Johnson's Dog," *Mennonite Quarterly Review* 71 (January 1977): 5–41.

6. Stuart Hirschberg, ed., *The Many Worlds of Literature* (New York: Macmillan, 1994), 96.

7. Jan Montefiore, *Feminism and Poetry: Language, Experience, Identity in Women's Writing* (London: Pandora Press, 1987).

8. Hirschberg, ed., *Many Worlds of Literature,* 97.

9. David Wojahn, "John Flanders on the Anxious Highway: First Books and the Politics of Poetry," *Writer's Chronicle* (March/April 2000): 26.

10. Unnamed reviewer, review of *Eve's Striptease* by Julia Kasdorf, in *Kirkus Reviews* (15 March 1998).

11. Personal letter in the collection of the author.

12. *Many Worlds of Literature Instructor's Manual* (New York: Macmillan, 1994), cited by John Kurtz, on menno.d@uci.com (3 January 1995).

13. J. Lorne Peachey, editorial, *Gospel Herald*, 17 January 1995, 16.

14. Gundy, "U.S. Mennonite Poetry," 7.

15. David Wright, "A New Mennonite Replies to Julia Kasdorf," *The Mennonite*, 25 May 1999, 5; used with permission.

16. For an excellent analysis and description of the sleeping preacher phenomenon, especially as it relates to the Amish community, see Steven D. Reschly, *The Amish on the Iowa Prairie, 1840 to 1910* (Baltimore: Johns Hopkins University Press, 2000), 132–57.

17. Antoine de Saint-Exupéry, *The Little Prince* (New York: Harcourt Brace Jovanovich, 1943), 70.

18. W. H. Auden, Introduction, in Adrienne Rich, *A Change of World* (New Haven: Yale University Press), 1951.

19. Virginia Woolf, *A Room of One's Own* (New York: Harvest / Harcourt Brace Jovanovich, 1981), 50.

6   Bodies and Boundaries

1. This image is used by Paton Yoder to illustrate the concept of *Gelassenheit* in his *Tradition and Transition: Amish Mennonites and Old Order Amish, 1800–1900* (Scottdale, Pa.: Herald Press, 1991), 80. In a footnote, Yoder cites this metaphor in a couple of Amish sermons and notes that Robert Friedmann traces it to the *Didache,* or "The Teaching of the Twelve Disciples," a document from the first or early second century A.D., introduced into Anabaptist discourse in the sixteenth century by Hans Hut (302).

The metaphor of the community as "one loaf" also appears in the third article of the Schleitheim Confession. J. C. Wenger alludes to this image: "The bread is spoken of as a loaf which symbolizes the spiritual unity of those who are in Christ." For Mennonites, he adds, the communion service "became so solemn as to be somber and heavy, with people often wearing dark clothes." He regrets this dreary turn, reminding readers that Menno Simons believed the supper should be "partaken of with holy joy" (*What Mennonites Believe* [Scottdale, Pa.: Herald Press, 1977], 36).

2. This is reported to have taken place in a 1931 Bible study class lecture on "Mennonite Youth in a Modern World." It appeared in the Goshen College newspaper (*Record,* October 1931), and was cited in Susan Fisher Miller's college history, *Culture for Service: A History of Goshen College 1894–1994* (Goshen, Ind.: Goshen College, 1994), 149.

3. George Lakoff and Mark Johnson, *Metaphors We Live By* (Chicago: University of Chicago Press, 1980) 14–15.

4. Simone de Beauvoir, *The Second Sex* (New York: Vintage Books, 1989), xxix.

5. The nature of Bakhtin's religious belief and practice have been the subject of debate for some time. Michael Holquist, in an introduction to a translation of Bakhtin's early work, writes, "It is well known that Bakhtin was, like his hero Dostoyevsky, a very complicated sort of Christian" (M. Holquist and Vadim Liapunov, eds., *Art and Answerability* [Austin: University of Texas Press, 1990], xxxix). In an essay tracing Russian Orthodox theological ideas in Bakhtin's early work, translator and Bakhtin biographer Caryl Emerson is less conclusive, locating the author's religious orientation somewhere between "a naive or proselytizing 'believer's theology'" and "a perfectly conventional German tradition, *Religionsphilosophie*" ("Russian Orthodoxy and the Early Bakhtin," *Religious Thought & Contemporary Critical Theory* [summer-autumn 1990]: 109, 113). More recently, an essay by Alan Jacobs concludes that new evidence from the former Soviet Union indisputably establishes Bakhtin's belief. Jacobs claims that many of Bakhtin's ideas are "undergirded," even "prompted," by rudimentary Christian doctrines ("The Man Who Heard Voices," *Books & Culture* [January/February 1996]: 26).

6. This statement was reported in *Hammer,* the newspaper of the Nevel Soviet of Workers, Peasants, and Red Army Deputies. See Sergy Bocharov, "Conversations with Bakhtin," *PMLA* 9, no. 5 (1994): 1021–22.

7. Bakhtin died in 1975, and an English translation of the essay I will consider was not published until 1990. Bakhtin's story parallels those of many Jews and German-speaking Christians who endured religious persecution and the pressures of Stalin's agricultural and social reforms. In 1929, the year of Bakhtin's exile, my father-in-law, Hans Kasdorf, a two-year-old still wearing dresses, left Siberia and emigrated to Germany and then to Brazil with a small band of Mennonite refugees.

8. For insight into these ideas, I am indebted, in particular, to conversations with Scott Holland, whose work places aesthetics prior to ethics, following the story of redemption wherein creation precedes the church. Moreover, this essay was written at Holland's invitation and owes a great deal to his writing and thought.

9. Holquist and Liapunov, *Art and Answerability,* 41–42.

10. Ibid., 51.

11. Pamela E. Klassen, *Going by the Moon and the Stars* (Waterloo, Ont.: Wilfrid Laurier University Press, 1994), 34–35.

12. Ibid., 80.

13. St. Augustine in his *Confessions* was among the earliest writers to compare the unfolding of a story with the living of a life. In recent years, feminist writers like Carolyn Heilbrun have made more explicit connections between the act of writing and the deliberate choices one makes in life, stressing the importance of stories that function as plots. In *Writing a Woman's Life* she writes, "We live our lives through texts. They may be read, or chanted, or experienced electronically, or come to us, like the murmuring of our mothers, telling us what conventions demand. Whatever their form or medium, these stories have formed us all; they are what we must use to make new fictions, new narratives" ([New York: Ballantine Books, 1988]), 37.

14. Holquist and Liapunov, *Art and Answerability*, 51.

15. Ibid, 57. In the Eastern tradition, it is believed that body and soul are deified together, so that whole and distinct beings interact with one another in paradise.

16. Dante, *The Paradiso*, trans. John Ciardi (New York: Penguin, 1970), 163–64.

17. Cited by Theron Schlabach, who has speculated that the popularity of singing schools in turn-of-the-twentieth-century Amish-Mennonite and Mennonite communities and the development of a tradition of four-part, a cappella congregational singing "probably shows something of how communal some Mennonite groups still were and how much they preferred blending over individualism" (*Peace, Faith, Nation* [Scottdale, Pa.: Herald Press, 1988], 70). And yet, traditional groups that opposed note-reading and harmony during this period argued that congregations should sing *in unison,* during worship services. Both positions seem to be struggling to negotiate the relationship between individual and communal voice. Is it more individualistic to sing only your part or to sing the same tune with everyone else?

18. Joseph W. Yoder, *Rosanna of the Amish* (Scottdale, Pa: Herald Press, 1978), 97.

19. Walter Ong, *Orality and Literacy* (New York: Routledge, 1989), 72–75.

20. *Prairie Fire* 11, no. 2 (summer 1990): 183; used with permission.

21. Emerson, "Russian Orthodoxy and the Early Bakhtin," 123.

7   Work and Hope

Epigraph: These are the final lines of "Freindschaft" in *Sleeping Preacher* (Pittsburgh: University of Pittsburgh Press, 1992), 21–23.

1. John S. Oyer and Robert S. Kreider, *The Mirror of the Martyrs* (Intercourse, Pa.: Good Books, 1990), 7.

2. I am thankful to Mervin Horst, who introduced me to the motto and later showed me a copy of the image.

3. Sandra Cronk discusses "the rite of work" as a means of creating community and expressing love in traditional communities in *"Gelassenheit:* The Rites and Redemptive Processes in Old Order Amish and Old Order Mennonite Communities," *Mennonite Quarterly Review* 60 (January 1981): 5–44.

4. In addition to the classic article by Gerald C. Studer, "A History of the *Martyrs Mirror,"* *Mennonite Quarterly Review* 22 (July 1948): 163–74; and *"Martyrs Mirror," Mennonite Encyclopedia,* 3:423–24, see John L. Ruth, *Maintaining the Right Fellowship* (Scottdale, Pa.: Herald Press, 1984); and E. G. Alderfer, *The Ephrata Commune: An Early American Counter Culture* (Pittsburgh: University of Pittsburgh Press, 1985), 127–29. Also see David Luthy's "The Ephrata *Martyrs Mirror:* Shot from Patriots' Muskets," *Pennsylvania Mennonite Heritage* 9 (January 1986), in which he describes the discovery of a copy of an Ephrata *Martyrs Mirror* that was among those confiscated by rebel soldiers during the American Revolution for use as musket wadding. Some feared that the war might be lost if the martyr books were used for this purpose, and Luthy's copy was among those returned to the cloister and later sold at a discounted price.

5. Cited in *Mennonite Encyclopedia,* 3:423.

6. Alderfer, *Ephrata Commune,* 16–26, 9, 48, 34, 48. *The Ephrata Commune* provides biographical information on Beissel and traces significant connections between the community at Ephrata and European mysticism, the German Pietist movement, contemporaneous colonial American religious activity, and later communal and religious movements in the United States.

7. *Güldene Aepffel in Silbern Schalen* (golden apples in silver bowls) was a 519-page devotional containing the "confession of faith by Thomas von Imbroich, and numerous other testimonials, epistles, prayers, and hymns by Mennonite martyrs" (Studer, "A History," 173). The cloister also published three editions of the prayer book *Die ernsthafte Christenpflicht* in 1745, 1770, and 1785, and at least one other catechetical tract for the Mennonites. For a complete descrip-

tion of Ephrata's printing for the Mennonites, see Alderfer, *Ephrata Commune,* 112, 127–29, 162, 168, 234.

8. Alderfer, *Ephrata Commune,* 86–106.

9. Lamech and Agrippa, *Chronicon Ephratense: A History of the Community of Seventh Day Baptists at Ephrata, Lancaster County, Pennsylvania,* trans. J. Max Hark (1889; reprint, New York: Burt Franklin, 1972), 214.

10. Samuel W. Pennypacker, "A Noteworthy Book: *Der Blutige Schau-Platz oder Nartyer Spiegel,* Ephrata, Pa., 1748," *Pennsylvania Magazine of History and Biography* 3 (1881), 287–88; cited in Luthy, "Ephrata *Martyrs Mirror,*" 4.

11. Lamech and Agrippa, *Chronicon Ephratense,* 210.

12. J. G. C. A. Briels, *Zuidnederlandse boekdrukkers en boekverkopers in de Nederlanded 1570–1630* (Nieuwkoop: de Graaf, 1974), 185. I am grateful to Joseph Springer, curator of the Mennonite Historical Library at Goshen College, for directing me to this and other reference materials and for sharing his insights into the possible sources of this image.

13. Bella C. Landauer, ed., *Printers' Mottoes* (New York: printed privately, 1926), n.p. Sem C. Sutter notes that the image can also be found in the emblem books common to seventeenth-century Europe: "In Henkel and Schone's *Emblemata,* column 1550 describes an emblem from a book by Gabriel Rollenhagen, *Selectorum emblematum centuria secunda* (Arnhem: Jassonius, 1913): *Spes mit dem Spaten grabend* (hope digging with a shovel) accompanied by the motto *Fac et spera* and a Latin verse meaning, 'Submit yourself to God by fulfilling the task given to you, and hope and ask for help in misfortune'" (Sutter to author, 27 April 1995). Since the completion of this article, a catalogue of Dutch printers' devices that includes many more examples and versions of the digging figure was released by P. Van Huisstede & J. P. J. Brandhorst in CD-Rom form with an Iconclass browser (*Dutch Printer's Devices 15th–17th Century* [Nieuwkoop: de Graaf, 1999]).

14. In the *Biblia Scara Mazarinaea* (Johann Gutenberg and Peter Schoeffer? 1454?) facsimile I consulted (Paris: Editions Les Incunables, 1985), a line-break falls after the phrase that may have served as the source of this motto: Spera in domino et fac / bonitatem et inhabita terram et pasceris in diuitiis eius.

15. Raimond Van Marle, *Iconographie de L'Art Profane au Moyen-Age et à la Renaissance et la Décoration des Demeures* (The Hague: Martinus Nijhoff, 1931), 1:373–98. Van Marle cites numerous examples and includes many photographs of rural life as depicted in European Medieval and Renaissance fine and decorative art.

16. Emil Male, *The Gothic Image: Religious Art in France of the Thirteenth Century,* trans. Dorea Nussey (New York: Harper & Row, 1972), 65.

17. Van Marle, *Iconographie,* 399–401.

18. Adriaan Plak, assistant curator of the Mennonite Library at the University of Amsterdam, who was very helpful to me on this project, recently discovered this image in a new acquisition of that collection. The print is unclear, apparently because many imprints were made from the woodblock, but it is not known where else the image may have been used. Plak, too, feels certain of a meaningful association between the figure on Braat's device and Adam after the Fall. In addition, a 1645 Dutch edition of *The Wandering Soul* shows the fallen Adam sitting on the ground next to a shovel, a plow, and a team of oxen.

19. Rolena Adorna, *Guaman Poma de Ayala: Writing and Resistance in Colonial Peru* (Austin: University of Texas Press, 1986), 100–102. Mary Louise Pratt also discusses this work in her essay on the power dynamics of crosscultural communication, "Arts of the Contact Zone," *Profession* 91 (MLA, 1991), which was subsequently reprinted as the introduction to her book, *Writing and Transculturation* (London: Routledge, 1992) and in *Ways of Reading,* ed. David Bartholomae and Anthony Petrosky (Boston: Bedford Books, 1993), 442–56.

20. Joseph Springer to writer, 30 November 1993.

21. David Luthy to writer, 7 December 1993.

22. The 1996 exhibition of material culture from these communities, "A Swiss Heritage in Decorative Arts," included a board with the painted motto, *An Gottes Segen ist alles gelegen,* which now belongs to the Swiss Community Historical Society of Bluffton and Pandora. The board was formerly attached to the east side of Peter Schumacher's barn, built in 1854 on Bixel Road between Bluffton and Pandora, and was said to have been removed in 1936. When the board entered the Society's collection, some older people recalled that another board, bearing the motto *Arbeite und Hoffe,* had been mounted on the west side of the barn. That board was never found; perhaps worn by wind and rain, which come mostly from the southwest, it may have been discarded. I am thankful to Ann Hilty of the Bluffton College gallery for drawing these boards to my attention on my visit to the exhibit and for later providing me with additional information.

23. *The Diary* 11 (July 1979). In his letter, David Luthy also quoted this line from *Liedersammlung B,* an 1860 collection of Amish songs probably compiled by Shem Zook, editor of the 1849 *Martyrs Mirror.* A version of the song can also

be found in an 1892 collection, *Liedersammlung G,* in which *Menschenkinder* is replaced by *Mein Kinder* (my children). The concept of "work and hope" for salvation is articulated in Psalm 119:116: "I hope for thy salvation, O Lord, and I do thy commandments."

24. John R. Renno, *A Brief History of the Amish Church in Belleville* (Danville, Pa.: author, ca. 1970), 21–22.

25. Joseph W. Yoder, *Rosanna's Boys* (Harrisonburg, Va.: Choice Publications, 1987 reprint), 248.

26. Calvin Redekop, *Mennonite Society* (Baltimore: Johns Hopkins University Press, 1989), 210.

27. Julia Kristeva, *Strangers to Ourselves* (New York: Columbia University Press, 1991), 18.

28. Quoted in John L. Ruth, *Mennonite Identity and Literary Art* (Scottdale, Pa.: Herald Press, 1978), 40.

29. "Migration of the 'Plain People' Revitalizes Farming," *New York Times,* 11 December 1993, Metro Section, 25, 29.

30. See Steven Nolt, "The Mennonite Eclipse," *Festival Quarterly* 19 (summer 1992): 8–11.

31. Telephone interview, 11 November 1992.

32. I. B. Singer and Richard Bargin, *Conversations with Isaac Bashevis Singer* (Garden City, N.Y.: Doubleday, 1985), 63.

33. This image was used on books printed in 1640, 1644, and 1659 titled *Onderwysinge in de Christelijcke religie ghestelt by vraghen ende antwoorden, na de belijdenisse der Remonstrants-Ghereformeerde Christenen. Midtsgaders der selfder formulieren ende ghebeden, des H. Droops ende des H. Avondtmaels.*

34. Leonard Byler, personal email, 19 January 1998.

8   Marilyn, H. S. Bender, and Me

1. The "Publisher's Preface to the Fifth English Printing, 1950," written in 1949 by Historical Committee member J. C. Wenger, traces the American printing history of *Martyrs Mirror,* which from the first colonial edition was used to "prepare their people for the cross of testing and suffering which war would bring with it." In reference to the midcentury edition, Wenger wrote, "Indeed the loyalty of the Mennonite brotherhood to its historic peace principles has been tested in the First and Second World Wars more severely than at any time since the sixteenth century. The pressures of the contemporary cul-

ture upon the group to surrender this historic principle are strong. It is evident that vigorous efforts must be made to capture the loyalty of our youth if the biblical doctrine of nonresistance is to be preserved" (in Thieleman J. van Braught, *The Bloody Theater or Martyrs Mirror* . . . , trans. Joseph F. Sohm (Scottdale, Pa.: Herald Press, 1977), n.p.

2. Gene Ringold, "Marilyn Monroe: Her Legend Triumphs Her Tragedy," *Screen Legends* (August 1965), 15.

3. I came across this line in the 1998 *Wild Women* desk calendar, and I have been unable to locate an adequate source for the quote. I have nonetheless chosen to include it because it seems to capture perfectly Marilyn's guileless public image, as Angela Carter has described it: "Because she is innocent of her exchange value, she thinks she is valueless" (*The Sadeian Woman and the Ideology of Pornography* [New York: Harper & Row, 1978], 66).

4. I have been unable to verify whether Bender actually mentioned Marilyn Monroe in his speech, and I now believe that he did not. William Klassen reports that neither the transcript nor the tape of the Sunday evening address include mention of Monroe, and Paul Tiessen speculates that Wiebe may have transferred the memory from a sermon at the Ottawa Street Mennonite Brethren church where the minister there, Tiessen recalls, explicitly referred to Marilyn's death. I repeat the story because it was told to me as true and I believe that it functions as a legend—an anecdote that is repeated and believed to be true although it may not be factual. Folklorists recognize that legends tend to fix on individuals with the greatest stature in a community, so it is understandable that the announcement would be attributed to Bender; and it is significant that the story seemed believable, or at least engaging enough to generate considerable discussion, when I first delivered this paper at Bluffton College in August 1998. I am grateful for the research of William Klassen and the folklorist instincts of Professor Ervin Beck in this matter.

5. "Our Witness for Nonconformity in Dress in the Future," Bender papers, quoted in Albert N. Keim, *Harold S. Bender, 1897–1962* (Scottdale, Pa.: Herald Press, 1998), 504.

6. *Mennonite Brethren Herald,* 16 August 1962, 5.

7. Ibid., 5.

8. Quoted in Carolyn G. Heilbrun, *Writing a Woman's Life* (New York: Ballantine Books, 1988), 109.

9. Paul Erb, *We Believe* (Scottdale, Pa.: Herald Press, 1969), 61–62.

10. Virginia Woolf, "Professions for Women," a paper prepared for and read to the Women's Service League, was published posthumously by Leonard Woolf in *Death of the Moth and Other Essays* (New York: Harcourt Brace, 1970), 237.

11. Ibid., 238.

12. *Mennonite Encyclopedia,* cited in *Mennonite Brethren Herald,* 24 August 1962, 1.

13. *Mennonite Brethren Herald,* 17 August 1962, 1.

14. The dissertation, suppressed by Bender and others at Goshen, was finally published along with responses in 1993: *The Limits of Perfection,* ed. Rodney J. Sawatsky and Scott Holland (Waterloo, Ont.: Institute of Anabaptist and Mennonite Studies).

15. *Mennonite Brethren Herald,* 10 August 1962, 1.

16. Rudy Wiebe, *Peace Shall Destroy Many* (Toronto: McClelland & Stewart, 1962), 8.

17. Ibid., 239.

18. Robert Bly, *A Little Book on the Human Shadow* (New York: HarperCollins, 1988), 23.

19. For example, I think of Sylvia Plath, for whom the year 1962 was famously productive. In October alone, she wrote twenty-five of the brilliant poems that would end up in *Ariel,* but by February of 1963, she had committed suicide, leaving two small children behind.

20. Woolf, "Professions," 241.

21. Ibid.

9   The Gothic Tale of Lucy Hochstetler and the Temptation of Literary Authority

1. Deputy Bontrager grew up in an Amish home in La Grange County, Indiana, although he later became an Episcopalian. A handwritten letter from an Amish person, now in the Samuel D. Hochstetler (1872–1954) file at the Mennonite Archives (Hist. Mss. 1-66), suggests that Bontrager's own troubled family history may have tainted his involvement in this case. Another document in this file suggests that as recently as 1994 members of the Hochstetler family seemed not to have known who reported the case to the authorities, and some suspected that it was a vengeful church member who took advantage of Mattie Troyer Hochstetler's recent death to implicate the bishop. During her investi-

gation of the case in the early 1990s, Mami Hiraike Okawara interviewed Bontrager and received from him an eighteen-page unsigned, undated, but handwritten account of the case, drawn from a document he had written years earlier. Bontrager's version seems finally to have become the most substantial and
authoritative source of information in Okawara's detailed interpretation of the
case, published in a 1997 article in the *Japanese Journal of American Studies* (no.
8), 119–41. This chapter owes a large debt to Okawara and also to Leonard Gross
of the Archives of the Mennonite Church, Goshen, Indiana, who assisted us
both.

2. Transcript, *State of Indiana* vs. *Samuel Hochstetler,* Elkhart Circuit Court,
February 1948, p. 8. This document can be found in the (Hist. Mss. 1-66)
Samuel D. Hochstetler (1872–1954) file.

3. Representative text from a photograph's caption is included below. In all
cases, the images appear to be posed. The captions stress that the photographs
were taken before Lucy was released, suggesting an interest in the sensational
shot that was prior to concern about her well-being. Bontrager's account of the
episode reveals that reporters also wanted to photograph the bishop behind
bars, but the deputy sheriff would not permit this.

From *The (Goshen) News-Democrat,* 23 January 1948:

Miss Lucy Hochstetler, 41, is shown above in the bed to which she had been
chained for three years in her parents' home several miles east of Goshen.
Holding one of the chains fastened to the woman's wrists is Sheriff Luther
W. Yoder. His deputy, Levi Bontrager, stands at the head of the bed and on
the opposite side of the bed, with his back to the camera is the woman's
father, Samuel D. Hochstetler, Amish bishop, who was sentenced to serve
six months, the maximum under the law, in the state penal farm for shack-
ling her.

4. This Japanese-Western difference was first described by Ruth Benedict in
her book *The Chrysanthemum and the Sword* (Boston: Houghton Mifflin, 1946).

5. Although there have been many others who have interpreted the case at
the time and afterward, these are the authors I wish to explore. For a contemporary Amish view of the case, see "Indiana Was Hasty," in Wayne L. Fisher,
The Amish in Court (New York: Vantage, 1996), 146–56.

6. This idea has been explored by Andrea Fishman in her ethnographic
study of Pennsylvania Amish literacy practices, *Amish Literacy: How and What
It Means* (Portsmouth, N.H.: Heinemann, 1988).

7. Goshen attorney Robert Hartzog was retained by Bishop Hochstetler's children to present the petition. One account sympathetic to the Amish position claims that Hartzog "volunteered to work with the family," and that the governor of Indiana owed Hartzog a favor, and so this personal connection figured into the decision. See Fisher, *Amish in Court,* 153, 155.

8. See Paul Toews, *Mennonites in American Society 1930–1970* (Scottdale, Pa.: Herald Press, 1996), 194–95, 173. Toews reports that, according to surveys conducted at the time, 53.7 percent of Mennonite men drafted into service opted for regular and noncombatant service. The remaining group opted for Civilian Public Service. The stories of Mennonites who served in World War II remain marginal in the group's memory due to ideological bias, and, Toews asserts, this reflects a general marginalization of those who defy the denominational position. Thus, it may be that the voiceless bodies during World War II were not the defenseless conscientious objectors but those Mennonite young men who survived or died in combat and whose story has been largely ignored by the community.

9. Yoder's letter of 25 January 1948 remains in the Yoder files of the Juniata College Archives in Huntingdon, Pennsylvania. The sheriff's reply to J. W. Yoder's letter, dated 28 January 1948, also in that file, was diplomatic and inconclusive. He referred to a "signed statement by a witness that Lucy wanted to leave the Amish People when she was about eighteen years of age," but he added that the family claimed she had showed signs of mental disturbance before then. "In other words," he wrote, "the cause of this sad condition is questionable."

10. Sandra Gilbert and Susan Gubar, *The Madwoman in the Attic* (New Haven: Yale University Press, 1979), 83–85.

11. Theron Schlabach, personal email, 4 September 1997.

12. The letters, dated 4 September 1994 and 30 October 1994, are in the personal files of the author.

13. Evan Boland, *Object Lessons: The Life of the Woman and the Poet in Our Time* (New York: W. W. Norton, 1995), 178.

14. "Some Amish Families Do Not Uphold Bishop Who Confined Daughter," La Grange newspaper clipping in J. W. Yoder files, Juniata College.

15. Boland, *Object Lessons,* 186.

10 Writing Like a Mennonite

1. Fred Kniss, *Disquiet in the Land: Cultural Conflict in American Mennonite Communities* (New Brunswick, N.J.: Rutgers University Press, 1997).

2. John Ruth in *Mennonite Identity and Literary Art* (Scottdale, Pa.: Herald Press, 1978) outlines the most obvious traditional resistances to literature among Mennonite peoples, including an amnesia of the oral literature resulting from the language shift from Pennsylvania German to English, and numerous religious and cultural scruples. Since the late 1970s, serious, imaginative literature by Mennonite writers has begun to blossom and has enjoyed both a popular reception and scholarly attention from Mennonite readers.

3. Thieleman J. van Braught, *The Bloody Theater or Martyrs Mirror . . .* , trans. Joseph F. Sohm (Scottdale, Pa.: Herald Press, 1977), 982.

4. Angela Carter, *The Sadeian Woman and the Ideology of Pornography* (New York: Harper and Row, 1978), 23.

5. John S. Oyer and Robert S. Kreider, *The Mirror of the Martyrs* (Intercourse, Pa.: Good Books, 1990), 13.

6. C. Arnold Snyder and Linda A. Huebert Hecht, eds., Introduction to *Profiles of Anabaptist Women* (Kitchener, Ont.: Canadian Corporation for Studies in Religion / Wilfrid Laurier University Press), 12.

7. Al Reimer, *Mennonite Literary Voices: Past and Present* (North Newton, Kans.: Bethel College Press, 1993), 15.

8. Judith Herman, M.D., *Trauma and Recovery* (New York: Basic Books, 1992), 83.

9. Pamela Klassen, *Going by the Moon and the Stars* (Waterloo, Ontario: Wilfrid Laurier University Press, 1994). See Marlene Epp, *Women Without Men: Mennonite Refugees of the Second World War* (Toronto: University of Toronto Press, 2000).

10. Other works of fiction were published by North American Mennonite writers before *Peace Shall Destroy Many,* but this book marks a turning point because it was regarded as a literary rather than a popular work, it explores Mennonite experience directly, it was broadly distributed, and it engaged readers both within and beyond the Mennonite community.

11. The essay originally appeared in the *Bulletin de la Société française de Philosophie* 63, no. 3 (1969), 73–104, and was first delivered as a lecture in 1969. "What Is an Author?" can be found in Michel Foucault, *Language, Counter-*

Memory, Practice: Selected Essays and Interviews, ed. and trans. Donald F. Bouchard (Ithaca: Cornell University Press, 1977).

12. Quoted in Oyer and Kreider, *Mirror of the Martyrs,* 9.

13. For several years during the early 1990s, Lois conducted a small discussion group of Mennonites who had grown up in conservative homes and who are successful in highly creative vocations. We met a few times a year for a full day at a time to reflect on our memories of the community and on the nature of creativity. Her initial hypothesis in this study was that the experience of being culturally marginal enables persons to function more creatively because they are used to being different and coping with issues of loneliness. Her research was reported in a paper delivered at The Quiet in the Land Conference (Millersville University, 1995) and later published as "Creativity: From Victim to Reconstructor," *Mennonot* 7 (spring 1996): 18–20.

14. Louise Glück, "The Idea of Courage," in *Proofs and Theories* (New York: Ecco Press, 1994), 25.

15. Hêlêne Cixous, *Three Steps on the Ladder of Writing* (New York: Columbia University Press, 1993), 21.

16. Dana Gioia, "To Witness the Truth Uncompromised: Reflections on the Modern Martyrs," *Image* 13 (Spring 96): 71–73.

17. Cixous, *Three Steps,* 36–37.

18. "The conflict between the will to deny horrible events and the will to proclaim them aloud is the central dialectic of psychological trauma" (Herman, *Trauma and Recovery,* 1).

JULIA SPICHER KASDORF was born in Lewistown, Pennsylvania, and is the author of two collections of poems: *Sleeping Preacher*, published in 1992, and *Eve's Striptease*, published in 1998. She published the biography *Fixing Tradition: Joseph W. Yoder, Amish American*, in 2002, and with Joshuah Brown edited Yoder's 1940 classic, *Rosanna of the Amish*, which appeared in 2008. In 2007, she published a poetry anthology titled *Broken Land: Poems of Brooklyn*, which she edited with Michael Tyrell. She is an associate professor of English and Women's Studies at the Pennsylvania State University.

CREDITS

Page 11: Personal collection. Page 13: Collection of the family. Page 14: Collection of the family. Page 20: Richard G. Hatton, *1001 Plant and Floral Illustrations: From Early Herbals* (New York: Dover Publications, reprint 1996), 161. Courtesy of Dover Pictorial Archive Series. Page 23: Richard G. Hatton, *1001 Plant and Floral Illustrations: From Early Herbals* (New York: Dover Publications, reprint 1996), 82. Courtesy of Dover Pictorial Archive Series. Page 28: Personal collection. Page 42: Personal collection. Page 49: David Kasdorf. Page 51: Uffizi, Florence, Italy. Giraudon/Art Resource, N.Y. Page 52: Carol Shadford. Page 53: Musée des Beaux-Arts, Dijon, France. Page 77: Sanford King. Page 88: Cay Lang. Page 94: *Passio Cristi ab Alberto Dürer Nurenbergense effigiata cū variis carminibus Fratis Benedicti Chelidonii Musophili* (Nuremberg, 1511), reprinted in *The Complete Woodcuts of Albrecht Dürer*, ed. Dr. Willi Kurth (New York: Dover Publications, 1963), fig. 253. Courtesy of Dover Pictorial Archive Series. Page 100: Thieleman J. van Braght, *Martyrs' Mirror*, trans. Peter Miller (Ephrata, 1748–49), title page. Page 101: Thieleman J. van Braght, *Martyrs' Mirror* (Amsterdam: J. vander Deyster, H. vanden Berg, Jan Blom, Wed. S. Swart, S. Wybrands, A. Ossaan, 1685), title page. Page 105: Thieleman J. van Braght, *Martyrs' Mirror* (Dordrecht: Jacob Braat, 1660), title page. Page 106: (top) Adriaen van Nispens, *Verscheyde Voyagien, ofte rysen . . .* (Dordrecht: Jacob Braat, 1652), title page. (bottom) Martin Tiele, *Das Ratsel des Emder Buchdrucks* (1554–1602) (Aurich, 1986). Page 108: (top) Darcy Lynn. (bottom) *L'Anabaptiste ou le Cultivateur par Expérience* (Belfort, France: J. P. Cleu, 1839), n.p. Page 109: (left) Jon Philippz Schabaelje, *De Vermeerderde Lustof des Gemoeds Met de Samenspraaken der Wandelande Ziele* (Amsterdam: Gysbert de Groot, 1692), 63. (right) *The First New Chronicle and Good Government*, in David Bartholomae and Anthony Petrosky, *Ways of Reading* (Boston: Bedford Books, 1993), 445. Page 110: Thieleman J. van Braght, *Martyrs' Mirror* (Lancaster, Pa.: Joseph Ehrenfried, 1814), title page. Page 111: Thieleman J. van Braght, *Martyrs' Mirror*, ed. Shem Zook (Philadelphia: King & Baird, 1849), title page. Page 112: Thieleman J. van Braght, *Martyrs' Mirror* (Elkhart, Ind.: John F. Funk und Bruder, 1870), title page. Page 116: Jerry Kearns and Palmer Museum of Art, The Pennsylvania State University. Page 117: *Mennonite Heritage Center Library and Archives* (Harleysville, Pa.: The MeetingHouse, 1990), pamphlet. Page 118: (top) Service Notice Series, New York City Metropolitan Transit Authority, 1994. (bottom) Julie Musselman. Page 119: *Onderwysinge in de Christelijcke . . .* (Hoorn: Isaac Willemsz van der Beeck, 1640), title page. Page 123: Mennonite Historical Library. Page 124: Copyright 1955. Twentieth Century Fox / Motion Picture & Television Photo Archive. Page 133: Hunsberger Photos, used by permission of *Mennonite Brethren Herald*. Page 135: Photographer unknown, from *Mennonite Brethren Herald*. Page 136: John H. Yoder Collection, Archives of the Mennonite Church, Goshen, Indiana. Page 147: Photograph and caption from a clipping in the J. W. Yoder papers at Juniata College. Page 148: *News-Democrat* (South Bend, Ind.) Friday evening edition, 23 January 1948. Photograph and caption from original newspaper clipping, Archives of the Mennonite Church, Goshen, Indiana, with permission of the photographer, W. W. Cooke Jr. Page 171: Thieleman J. van Braght, *Martyrs' Mirror* (Amsterdam, 1685), reprinted in John S. Oyer and Robert S. Kreider, *The Mirror of the Martyrs* (Intercourse, Pa.: Good Books, 1990), 24. Page 186: Thieleman J. van Braght, *Martyrs' Mirror* (Amsterdam, 1685), reprinted in John S. Oyer and Robert S. Kreider, *The Mirror of the Martyrs* (Intercourse, Pa.: Good Books, 1990), 52.

9 780271 035444